ON BEING A TEACHER

Other books on higher education by the same author :

The Higher Learning in India, edited alongwith Philip G. Altback, 1973

The Management of Examinations, edited alongwith H.S. Singha, 1976

University and College Finances, edited alongwith G.D. Sharma, 1980

Asking for Trouble: What It Means to be a Vice-Chancellor Today, 1984

Commonsense About Examination, 1984

Redeeming Higher Education: Essay in Educational Policy, 1985

Higher Education in India: The Social Context, edited alongwith G.D. Sharma, 1988

Higher Education in India: The Institutional Context, edited alongwith G.D. Sharma, 1989

ON BEING A TEACHER

Edited by
Amrik Singh

KONARK PUBLISHERS PVT LTD

KONARK PUBLISHERS PVT LTD
A-149, Main Vikas Marg, Delhi 110092

Copyright © Editor, 1990

Lasertypeset at Excel Computer Services, New Delhi and printed at Shiba Offset Printing Press, Delhi - 110092

*Dedicated to the memory of
Dr Zakir Hussain,
a teacher who was always proud of his profession*

List of Contributors

BHABATOSH DATTA is one of the senior economists of the country and continues to be Professor Emeritus at Presidency College, Calcutta.

ANDRE BETEILLE is Professor of Sociology at the University of Delhi.

J.N. KAPUR retired as Professor of Mathematics from IIT, Kanpur and is Professor Emeritus both at the University of Delhi and the IIT, Delhi.

M.V. PYLEE retired as Vice-Chancellor of Cochin University and is currently an industrial consultant.

M.S. GORE has been Vice-Chancellor both of the Tata Institute of Social Sciences, Bombay and the University of Bombay.

C.T. KURIEN was Principal of Madras Christian College when he wrote this piece. Currently he is Director of the Madras Institute of Development.

V. RAJAGOPALAN was Vice-Chancellor of Tamil Nadu Agricultural University, Coimbatore.

C.D. SIDHU teaches English at Hans Raj College, Delhi.

KRANTI JUJREKAR teaches Chemistry at Siddharth College, Bombay.

D.N. WAKHLU was Principal of the Regional Engineering College, Srinagar when he wrote this piece.

MADHU KISHWAR teaches English at Satyavati Co-educational College, Delhi. She is also editor of the well known women's magazine 'MANUSHI'.

UPENDRA BAXI was Professor of Law at the University of Delhi and also Research Director at the Indian Law Institute, New Delhi. Since he wrote the piece, he has been appointed Vice-Chancellor, University of Delhi.

SURESH C. GOEL was a Professor of Biological Sciences at the Indira Gandhi National Open University, New Delhi at the time of his death in 1989.

AMRIK SINGH is the editor of this volume.

W.H. McLEOD is Professor of History at the University of Otago, New Zealand. Apart from teaching in India, he has also taught in Sussex, Berkeley and Toronto.

Contents

1. Introduction — 1
   Amrik Singh

2. The Adventure of Teaching — 13
   Bhabatosh Datta

3. A Career in a Declining Profession — 30
   Andre Beteille

4. A Personal Narrative — 47
   J.N. Kapur

5. Looking Back — 59
   M.V. Pylee

6. A Cause and an Opportunity — 70
   M.S. Gore

7. In Search of Relevance — 79
   C.T. Kurien

8. The Pleasure of Being a Teacher — 98
   V. Rajagopalan

9. In Search of Authenticity — 104
   C.D. Sidhu

10. Grappling with Problems — 120
    Kranti Jujrekar

11. Walking on Water — 131
    D.N. Wakhlu

12. Scattering the Seeds 142
    Madhu Kishwar

13. Teaching as Provocation 150
    Upendra Baxi

14. Sincerity in Teaching 159
    Suresh C. Goel

15. On Being a Teacher 173
    Amrik Singh

16. Teaching History to Undergraduates in India: A Trans-Indian View 190
    W.H. McLeod

INDEX 205

Introduction

OVER the years, almost every teacher comes to develop some kind of a philosophy and technique about the job in which he is engaged. Whether he is aware of it or not, he has an undefined notion in his mind with regard to the purpose and mode of teaching. It is not every one, however, who can articulate for himself what he has arrived at. This is because while some people are articulate and in a position to define and describe what they are guided by, others are not as well endowed or lack the inclination and the urge to do so.

Having said this, it would perhaps clarify things further if it were to be explained how this book came to be put together. It was sometime at the end of 1984 that the University Grants Commission and the National Institute of Educational Planning and Administration collaborated with the UNESCO to organise a seminar on the Methodologies of Teaching. I was asked to contribute to it. Till the moment I was asked, it was not clear to me what I wanted to say. However, over the weekend, I wrote the piece 'On Being a Teacher' which appears in this volume under my name. Looking back, it appears that what I did in this piece was to articulate in a somewhat unsystematic manner whatever I had thought and reflected about the art of teaching.

Having done so, I felt rather pleased about it. When I wrote this piece, I was no longer involved in active teaching though, to be sure, there were occasions when I was required to lecture to various kinds of audiences. The teaching strategies that I had evolved for myself helped me to perform better than might have been the case otherwise. In any case, what I had done was to analyse what I had learnt for myself. There had been no books to learn from and no guidance of any kind. In a sense, it was a signal example of the trial and error method. Years later, when I did come upon a few books and articles, it was more a case of confirmation than discovery. Indeed it was a source of satisfaction to find that without my knowing it, I had followed the right track, or almost so.

While all this was gratifying, it occurred to me that though I had come across a few books dealing with the art of teaching, almost all of them were based on non-Indian experience. I started looking for something which was based on our own experience. It was astonishing, to say the least, that there was hardly any book available on this subject. More or less as an extension of this feeling of curiosity, I started looking for books which dealt with the problems of teaching at the school level. There also the situation was equally unsatisfactory.

A few things were available but none of them was characterised either by insight or lucidity. One or two books which I came across in Indian languages were more satisfactory from this point of view that they at least based themselves on indigenous experience. From this somewhat disconcerting discovery, it was only a short step to ask some people I had known in the course of my academic career to similarly reflect over the path of self-discovery as teachers that they had traversed. The response was good. Half a dozen persons responded in positive terms.

Meanwhile I published my own piece and started looking for other persons whom I did not know but who had a reputation as teachers. Some of them were vaguely known to me while in the case of others I discovered them through a circuitous path. Altogether more than 50 persons were asked to write on this theme. Almost half of them have done so and the result is here for the readers to judge for themselves. Some pieces which deal more with the strategies of teaching are proposed to be published separately. This particular volume is focussed on what it means to be a teacher.

II

While asking different persons to write on this theme I had three considerations in mind. The first one was that they should have had something like 15 years of experience of teaching. It takes that much time to evolve into a mature teacher. One has to have experience of different types of students in different settings and at different levels of understanding. The wider the range of experience, the more swiftly a teacher matures. There was also another angle to it.

Most persons in India as elsewhere begin their teaching in their middle 20's. By the time they are either 40 or so, they are at a stage of life where they have either entered or are about to enter their middle age. In most cases they have families and children. Put another way, in generational terms, they are no longer what they were when they entered the profession. For their part they have moved away somewhat from the young people with whom they interact everyday.

At the same time they are not so distant from them as not to be able to understand or empathise with them. In a sense, therefore, they are in their mid career and by then most of them have evolved both a philosophy and a strategy of teaching. It should not be necessary to repeat therefore that none of the contributors to this volume has less than 15 years of experience as a teacher.

Secondly, it was important to ensure that the contributors belonged to different university disciplines. Every discipline has its own imperative and that shapes and determines, at least to some extent, how the concerned teacher approaches the task of teaching. It was important to ensure this diversity of background. Unless that was done, the volume was likely to appeal to a limited audience and not the entire spectrum of academics as it is intended to.

Thirdly, the book is addressed both to college and university teachers. In one sense the problems of undergraduate and postgraduate teaching are different. But in another sense there are good many similarities. In any case, quite a number of teachers operate at more than one level. This is not to overlook a very substantial segment of the teaching community which is exclusively involved in undergraduate teaching. Perhaps in terms of numbers they would be more than 50 per cent of the total strength. Nonetheless, quite a few of them have a considerable measure of interest in what happens at the other level; and that had to be taken into account.

The problems of research are not referred to directly but quite a number of contributors do refer to them. For obvious reasons, the focus of the book is on teaching and not on research. Since teaching is closely allied to research and a certain percentage of teachers do engage in research, this issue could not but come up for consideration. In any event, the link between teaching and research had to be underlined and it has been appropriately underlined by several of the contributors.

III

It is not an accident that, as stated above, hardly anything has been written about the art of teaching in our country. From this it does not follow that we do not have competent and committed teachers. But for the presence of a substantial number of such teachers, the system could not have functioned. Even today when the system is under severe stress, quite a proportion of those engaged in teaching are doing their job very well. It is difficult to estimate what is the proportion of persons who perform indifferently or poorly. Everybody has his own guess. My guess is that, local variations apart, the proportion of such people is less than one quarter of the total strength. This could be wrong. In any case, the situation varies from place to place and state to state.

What is important is not to work out a correct estimate which in any case cannot be worked out. What is important is to worry about that fairly high proportion of teachers who do not perform as well as they should. While some of them are presumably too apathetic and too uninvolved in what they are doing, everyone is not like that. More particularly, recruitment into the profession has improved of late. Consequently the proportion of those who wish to do their job seriously as well as competently is increasing. They need to be helped and this book is a modest contribution towards that objective.

There are various ways of helping teachers to improve their teaching capabilities. Workshops and seminars, mostly based on a particular discipline, have been organised for a number of years. Those who participate in them do profit from their participation to some extent. At any rate they get to know more about their discipline than they did before their participation. To some extent they also discover the gaps in their knowledge and understanding. In their own way they try to fill in those gaps. To what extent they succeed or do not succeed depends partly upon their individual initiative and partly on the academic circumstances in which they have to operate. It should not be necessary to say anything more on this subject except to make a passing reference to the recent establishment of approximately 50 Academic Staff Colleges which have been sponsored and funded by the UGC.

While enhanced knowledge about the subject is important, it is no less important that teachers also get answers to questions like the following. What are the objectives of teaching? How do these vary from one level of teaching to another level? How are these objectives

Introduction

to be fulfilled? What is expected of the teacher as well as the student? How does a teacher arouse and sustain the interests of his student? In what manner do students differ from one another and from one level to another? In what circumstances do students respond as the teacher wishes them to respond and what makes them lose interest in what is being done in the classroom? How should a teacher prepare for the class? How useful is the lecture method and to what use can the various other methods of teaching be put? What is the role of physical and other facilities in the choice of the various methods? Not only that, which method is useful at which stage and in what proportion? Can these various methods be combined? If so, then with what degree of success?

There are scores of such questions which every teacher has to ask himself and find answers to. Sometimes he is helped by some of his colleagues and seniors but, more often than not, he has to fumble through on his own. There is hardly any guidance available. Nor is the relevant kind of literature accessible or even available. In such a situation what does an average teacher do? He relies upon his own resources and wits.

Sometimes he recalls what his own teacher used to do. But more often than that, he relies upon his ability to improvise and his love of his students. This last factor needs to be emphasised. If one has love for one's students and has their interest at heart, an average teacher, however untutored he might be, manages to perform, and gradually learns the craft. Though there is a good deal that can be said in disagreement with this statement, all said and done, teaching is a craft that, like any craft, can and requires to be learnt. The purpose of this book is to help those who have such questions in their minds and do not know how to find answers to them.

IV

It would be misleading to claim that one has only to know the art of teaching and, as a consequence, good teaching would follow. Good teaching is the outcome of several factors at work. Competence in one's chosen discipline is of course the basic prerequisite. To have acquired the art of teaching and enhanced one's capability helps as, in the obverse, its lack cripples one to quite an extent. Secondly, love of one's students and interest in teaching are equally important prerequisites. The act of teaching implies the desire to impart knowledge. The imparting of knowledge, if it is done with a sense of genuineness and commitment, fills the teachers with a sense of joy. He is happy only when he is teaching. The element of joy is also there even as he is learning more and more in order to be able to teach. But the overriding objective is how to be able to teach, and indeed teach effectively.

Thirdly, there is a distinction implied here between teaching and research. One may be a good teacher but not a good researcher and vice versa. Instances are not unknown where both qualities are not to be found in the same person. But quite a number of teachers do possess both these qualities. That is one reason why it is argued repeatedly, and not without reason, that teaching and research go together. Ideally speaking, they should go together. But there are situations when the two are not found in the same person. That fact too must be acknowledged and allowed for.

The distinction drawn above however implies one thing. If someone knows that he is interested in research and not in teaching, he would be well advised not to take up a teaching job. It can be no one's contention that one is superior to the other. The chief difference between a teacher and a researcher is that a teacher is genuinely and deeply interested in the imparting of knowledge as well as human interaction whereas a researcher's main interest is in ideas and discoveries. Once in a while one comes across individuals who are misfits, either in one category or the other. But those are exceptional cases, relatively speaking, and one need not attach too much importance to such cases. But this much should be understood clearly that it is different qualities of mind and personality which are called into play in the job of teaching as distinct from that of a researcher.

Even when all the favourable factors listed above are found in a particular individual, it does not follow that this will lead to good teaching. For that objective to be achieved another vital ingredient must be there, and this refers to professionalism. There is something odd about the profession of teaching in our country. In one sense it is profession. In another sense it is not yet exactly a profession for the simple reason that a sense of professionalism has not yet fully developed in the situation in which we operate.

V

Strictly speaking, professionalism implies three things. One is a long and somewhat arduous period of preparation and training. In order to enter the profession of college or university teaching, every one is required to have studied for a minimum period of 15 years. After that he is expected, and now required, to get his M. Phil. and then his Ph. D. From this point of view, therefore, the first condition is met.

The second condition is that there has to be a distinct sense of professional competence and professional pride. As any one concerned with the academic profession can see for himself, the situation in this regard is less than satisfactory. A certain measure of professional competence in respect of quite a large number of people does exist. But what is called professional pride is a rare phenomenon. This is not to suggest that those who are committed to teaching lack in professional pride. But, as stated above, their proportion is not very high.

Professional pride is to some extent an outcome of recognition by others, both by one's peers and others in society. In the manner in which the profession has evolved, the judgement by one's peers is either weak or non-existent. At any rate it is influenced by subjective and other questionable factors. As to the recognition accorded by the society, things are not too encouraging and that is why even those who have good reasons to feel proud of what they are doing do not always feel so.

It is in respect of the third condition that the situation is highly unsatisfactory. One mark of a good professional is that a substantial part of his satisfaction comes from the feeling of a job well done. In plain words, unless a teacher has a sense of satisfaction on the basis of what he is doing, there is something wrong somewhere. His reward is not only the emoluments and facilities which he gets. Those, it goes without saying, have to be satisfactory. But his real reward is from a job well done. It is here that the profession of teaching is at its weakest and it is here that a drastic change is called for.

Perhaps there would be no drastic change in the near future. It will take place not only within teaching but in respect of the wider social concerns in the midst of which we operate. This is only a way of saying that teaching too is today affected by poor and indifferent performance as other walks of life.

Having said this, however, it requires to be added that this is only a part of the explanation. A question which every one in the profession has to ask is if he is performing as well as he can and how does he compare with his counterparts in other parts of the world. This is because knowledge is universal in character.

Those who are engaged in the dissemination of knowledge cannot but perform on the same plane on which others are performing. A teacher of physics, for instance, is in an indirect and, even unstated, competition with a teacher of physics in any other country. No one who is engaged in teaching can protect himself against the charge of underperformance by referring to difficulties and distortions that may exist here and there. But the fact remains that he is to be judged in relation to what his counterparts are doing in other countries.

The moment one applies this yardstick to the profession of teaching, one can see where the problem lies. It would be presumptuous to claim that any attempt, however ambitious, can bring about an outlook and orientation which it is essential to bring about. But any kind of attempt which awakens the general body of teachers to the need for doing so and provides some guidelines, however limited those might be, is a step in the right direction.

One more dimension also needs to be referred to. Competence in one's profession is expected of everyone who chooses to opt for a professional career. This becomes immediately clear if we apply this criterion to a doctor or a surgeon. Are we prepared to accept his lack of competence on the ground that performance in other walks of life is poor? Our immediate response would be to panic, for what is at stake is our life. If we reject underperformance there, should we be prepared to accept it in teaching?

VI

Of the various explanations which can be advanced to explain the sorry state of the profession of teaching, perhaps the most obvious is the absence of professionalism. What professionalism implies has been briefly described above. It should not be necessary to go over the same ground once again. But before this issue is discussed further, one fallacy should be got out of the way.

Introduction

Teachers at the college and university level today are not in the same plight as they were a couple of decades ago. Then things were very bad. After two revisions of pay scales, the situation is much more satisfactory than it was visualised at one time. Facilities like housing etc. are still poor. What those in the government and the private sector get is distinctly better but for the rest the situation has visibly improved. In consequence the quality of people who now opt for teaching has also started improving.

It should not be necessary to pursue this line of argument any further. At one time low wages and poor performance were seen to be linked to each other. Now, wages have improved but performance has not improved. Two reasons for it can be identified. One of them is the overwhelming presence of such people who should never have got into teaching but, because of the extraordinary expansion that took place, they got into teaching and now the system does not know how to turn its back on them. Nor does it know how to help them to grow. This part of the problem is without question difficult to solve.

But the second related aspect, absence of professionalism, is a serious handicap and needs to be overcome. What is more, it is possible to do so. A precondition for it, however, is that the initiative must come from within the profession and that is precisely what is not happening.

In this connection, the data collected by Rais Ahmed in regard to scientific research in institutions of higher learning may be referred to. While only an interim report has been published and the full study is yet to follow, the data collected so far depicts a sad situation and requires to be noted.

According to the researchers, 30 per cent of the supervisors do not devote enough time to them, 40 per cent do not actually 'participate' in research and 30 per cent do not care to check experimental data which will ultimately bear their name. Another 40 per cent of the scholars have complained that their supervisors are not generous in giving them credit for what they do.

In regard to the prevalent academic values, the situation is downright unsatisfactory. Asked that they would do if the Ph. D. thesis which they were asked to examine was based on unsound concepts, used inappropriate methodology and wrong or unsound analysis, only 9-15 per cent replied that they would reject the thesis. A good 30-40 per cent were in favour of awarding the degree nonetheless. As many as 50 per cent were so 'kind' that they would be prepared to recommend that the thesis be revised. Clearly, these supervisors lack what is called academic integrity or the rigour of judgement that goes with it.

Yet another question asked of the researchers was if they faced any kind of prejudice or discrimination on the basis of sex, caste, religion and domicile. Half of them replied that that was precisely their experience. How many of them manipulated or forged data in respect of the research projects in which they were engaged? Their response to this question too was highly damaging. One third of those in the central universities replied that they manipulated data occasionally while those in the state universities and IITs thought that this happened in one quarter of cases. A small percentage admitted to indulging in this malpractice frequently and as many as 15-23 per cent did not choose to respond.

Manipulation of data is bad enough. To forge it is however much more deplorable. When asked, one quarter of those in the central universities admitted to occasionally doing so whereas the percentage in other institutions was lower. Several more such damaging admissions are made. When linked up with the earlier formulation that a substantial number of supervisors do not feel involved in what those registered under them are doing, the inference is obvious. A large number of them do not act with that degree of professional competence and integrity which is required of them.

There is so much more in this survey which could be quoted to make the point that, more than anything else, it is lack of professionalism which is responsible for what happens in our laboratories and classrooms. Normally speaking, it is difficult to prove whether somebody is professional or unprofessional. Most persons evade answering inconvenient questions. Once in a while the true situation gets disclosed. Those who feel bothered by such disclosures then attempt to explain away the findings.

This is precisely what happened in 1982 when a research study sponsored by the Association of Indian Universities established, with the help of official record, that in a prestigious college in Delhi all that the teachers did was to meet about a hundred classes in a year as against more than a thousand that they were required to do. The data

Introduction

could not be controverted because it had been made available by the college itself. Therefore, the next best thing was done and that was to explain away what had been happening as an aberration or something that happened in a given set of circumstances and so on.

One need not probe these issues any further. What happens in our educational institutions is not a secret. Almost every one is an accomplice in the game. This includes students, teachers, administrators as also the society at large. Even the parents who have a direct stake in the matter do not always intervene in favour of higher standards of performance.

This is not the occasion to discuss these issues at any length. These details have been brought up to underline the point that the absence of professionalism is such a compelling reality that inconvenient data, if assembled, is sought to be brushed away instead of a candid admission that things are unfavourable and need to be corrected. The very attempt to deny inconvenient facts is an indication of what is wrong with the profession.

VII

To what extent is professionalism conditioned by what happens in the rest of the society? The question is worth asking for one simple reason. Unable to defend poor performance or underperformance, a large number of teachers seek to explain away the situation in terms of what is happening all around us. Since performance in other sectors of life is poor, it is argued that the same level of performance, if encountered in higher education, need not be regarded as unnatural or indefensible.

There is something to this point of view. But what it overlooks is that a profession is judged in terms of the norms it lays down for itself and not in terms of what others say about it. That is what is distinctive about professionalism. Its norms of performance are not laid down by others. On the contrary those are laid down by the practitioners themselves. A profession in that sense is independent, autonomous and self-regulating.

Does the teaching profession answer this description? It does not and that is precisely the problem. As stated earlier, teaching has been in the process of becoming a profession for a long time. By the same token, it has not yet become a profession. Had the circumstances been favourable the process need not have taken as long as it has. In fact, the process has been at work for over four decades. Instead of the situation getting crystallised during these few decades, the between and betwixt position has got unconscionably prolonged with the result that there are people who would argue that the situation today is, in certain respects, worse than what it was some decades ago.

While it may be worse in certain respects, it also needs to be acknowledged that in certain other respects it is better. To the extent that it is better, it is because of a higher degree of professionalism. To the extent that it is poorer than before, it is because of the absence of professionalism. This is something so obvious and so incontestable that not to recognise this fact would be to fly in the face of experience.

Professionalism is, thus, the key to whatever might be planned in respect of the academic renovation of our institutions of higher learning. As part of that commitment to professionalism, every one who is engaged in teaching has to perform better. Better performance means better teaching and better research output. Since in this book we are concerned with better teaching, let it be also added that better teaching is not something that takes place on its own or without preparation or planning. Whatever else preparation or planning may imply, an unavoidable part of it is to learn the art of teaching. This particular volume is calculated to help those who are entering the profession or have been in the profession for some time.

One word about the dedication of this book. It is dedicated to the memory of a man whom I met only once but never got to know. His example, however, has influenced me most profoundly. It may be recalled in this connection that when he was sworn in as the President of the country, Dr. Zakir Hussain observed: "I may be forgiven the presumption that my choice to this office has mainly, if not entirely, been made on account of my long association with the education of my people." Nothing could have revealed the man more decisively than this simple and sincere statement. The least that we in the profession can do is to recall his work and personality with a sense of gratitude. It was something to have been his contemporary and to have looked upon him as a model.

AMRIK SINGH

July 1, 1990

2
The Adventure of Teaching

BHABATOSH DATTA

BEING a teacher has been a multi-splendoured adventure. It is a story of growth comprising a wide variety of facets. The story of my growing up as a teacher started from my childhood. The only life I knew as a child was that in a college teacher's family. My father taught Chemistry and Botany all through his working life—at Patna, Daulatpur (Khulna), Mymensingh and Dacca, the last three of which are now in Bangladesh. His younger brother, my own brother and sister and six of my first cousins taught in different colleges in Bengal, including Presidency College and the University of Calcutta.

Teaching was in a sense in my blood and when I myself entered the set, I knew I was where I should be. I did try for one or two other types of jobs, but fortunately failed to get any. I took my first degrees during the bottom of the Great Depression and I could not therefore be particularly choosy. But I was lucky and got an offer for joining a temporary lecturer's post within two months of my passing the Master's examination. The family tradition was maintained, but I had to explore my own path to grow in my own way.

I was born almost within the precincts of the Bihar National College at Patna, where my father had started his life as a college lecturer. He then came to a famous residential college—the Hindu Academy at Daulatpur, Khulna— and I grew up in one of the houses on one side of the college playground, the other sides of which were occupied by the main college building and the students' hostels. I followed the seasonal changes—the coming of the new students in July-August, the college sports and Saraswati Puja in the winter, the examinations in March-April and the visits by dignitaries all throughout the year.

The Sadler Commission came when I was six years old and my most clear memory is that of Sir Asutosh Mukherjee. I also remember one fat Englishman who, I was told, was the Director of Public Instruction. I was over-awed, but did not know then that I would have to experience the travails of that office later in my life. One of the visits I remember clearly is that of Lord Ronaldshay, who devoted nearly a full chapter on this visit in his book *The Heart of Aryavarta*. Daulatpur left a lasting impression on me. When much later in my life I saw Santiniketan for the first time, I remembered Daulatpur with its sprawling campus, its trees and low buildings, its ascetic standards and its camaraderie. In my inmost heart, I have always had a longing to teach at a college like Daulatpur, but that was not to be.

My father left Daulatpur when I was ten years old and then spent practically the whole of his life teaching at Dacca. I attended school there and did my Intermediate from my father's college. He had a strong fascination for Presidency College and disregarding the existence of a full-fledged University at Dacca itself, he sent me to Presidency for my B.A. Honours in Economics. That was a decision for which I have remained for ever grateful to him, for Presidency College gave me a character and a vision which only a college of its great traditions could give.

When I myself became a teacher, I knew that the conditions would not be replicated elsewhere, but I knew also that once a teacher is within the classroom, the empathy between him and his students would enable him to build his own path. There were models of teachers to follow—Phani Bhusan Chakravarti at Jagannath College, Dacca, Jehangir Coyajee and Prafulla Chandra Ghosh at Presidency and Jitendra Prasad Niyogi and Benoy Kumar Sarkar at the University of Calcutta. But every teacher has to shape his own evolution, gaining from his environment, from his colleagues and from the intellectual provocation received from intelligent students.

Such provocation I received in plenty. I was twenty-one years old when I started teaching and fiftyone when I left this track for other assignments. During this thirty-year period, ranging from 1932 to 1962, I had a varied experience of college teaching—in small colleges and in large ones, in Calcutta colleges and in colleges in the districts, in government colleges and in private colleges, in the University of Calcutta—and also over the whole spectrum, from intermediate to postgraduate classes.

My first appointment was in a four-month leave vacancy at the

The Adventure of Teaching

Chittagong College, followed by nearly two years at the Burdwan Raj College. After that I came to Ripon College (now Surendranath College) in Calcutta and taught there for eight years. Then I entered government service and was posted at the Islamia College, Calcutta (now Maulana Azad College). My last and longest teaching appointment was at Presidency College, where I worked till 1962. Most of the time I was teaching in the postgraduate classes of the University also.

II

This varied experience helped me to grow not only as a teacher, but also as a person. Chittagong in 1932 was a troubled town. Two extremist challenges against the British power had taken place in quick succession—the Armoury Raid in 1930 and the raid on the European Club in 1932. Revolution was in the air and it was not a very secure place for a youngman, even though he was serving in a government college. The army patrols could at any time ask him to raise his hands and get searched.

Because of my age, I was not permitted to use a bicycle. But the college was remarkably quiet and the students courteous and understanding. I had to join at very short notice and when I found myself inside a classroom, I had to ask the students where I was expected to begin. I was the only teacher of my subject in the college. The students who were only three years younger than me, helped me enthusiastically and I started to talk. I then discovered that I could talk.

I still cherish fond memories of Chittagong where I felt decisively that I would be able to make myself useful to my students. Burdwan was a contrast. It did not have the facilities that a government college could provide and had to depend on the charity of the Maharaja's estate. But I was lucky in my colleagues and students. And as I lived with the students in their hostel, my contact with them outside the classrooms was valuable to me. They came to me with problems of economics and also with their personal problems.

For the first time in my life, I came in contact with a feudal and rural society in which the urge for education had often to play a second role, with other pressures dominating. Neither Chittagong nor Burdwan had any Honours class in Economics but the students allowed their young enthusiastic teacher to go much beyond the Pass Course, even when they knew that they did not require all that for earning their degree. A degree had a great value in the somnolescent rural society of Burdwan.

And then I came to Ripon College in Calcutta. It was a remarkable institution with three thousand students and with a performance record of some seventy per cent failure combined with another record of some ten or twelve students taking the top places in the Intermediate examination every year. These students were attracted to the college partly because of the liberal concessions and stipends granted by the authorities and partly also because the college had a very high reputation in teaching.

The Principal, Rabindra Narayan Ghosh, was a great scholar. He could persuade the governing body—almost fully controlled by the heirs of the founder, Surendranath Banerjea—to appoint persons without any consideration of avuncular pressures and other extraneous factors. In the eight years I spent there, I had as my colleagues, brilliant litterateurs like Buddhadeva Bose, Ajit Datta, Bishnu Dey and Pramathanath Bisi, outstanding historical scholars like Hiren Mukherjee (he was to become a famous M.P. later), first-rate teachers of English like Birendra Benod Roy, Humphry House and Nripendra Chatterjee, in addition to Principal Ghosh himself and the internationally famous mathematician Nandalal Ghosh. We were all young then and looking back I feel that to be young in the nineteen-thirties in such a company was truly heaven.

I learnt much more from my colleagues than I could ever learn from books. They talked about modern literature and art, about current politics, about philosophy and science and everything else on earth. Sometimes the senior teachers would join us and Principal Ghosh would quietly make incisive comments on some of our views, but we the younger people felt confident of ourselves. Our incomes were low, but one could purchase three 'Penguins' for a rupee and see the latest film at the best of the houses for six annas.

And then there were the students. The general body was made up of candidates taken in indiscriminately—the college could not afford to lose the fees they paid—but inside the classroom they were admirably serious. The classes—except those in the Honours papers—were at least 150 strong and we had to strain our vocal chords to the furthest limit. It was not simply that the numbers were large, there was the more difficult problem of holding classes in a building located at the junction of one of the most noisy streets of Calcutta and a crowded bazar lane with historical links with Job Charnock. Sealdah Station was only a furlong away and the Sadler Commission had reported that two colleges near the railway station did not have any students' common room, but the large waiting hall of the station served the purpose.

There was more than one section for most of the courses and lectures had to be repeated. A very interesting feature was the 'plucked sections' which enrolled only the repeaters and their number was many. There were some among them who were trying their third or fourth chances. In the 'plucked section' for the final year B.A. students, there were obviously some students older than many of us. But they treated us with good humour and sometimes flattered us by comparing the teaching at Ripon College with what they had seen and heard in other institutions.

Teaching three or four hours a day (an 'hour' meant 45 minutes and, in effect, less) in classes of 150 compelled us to discover for ourselves the right way to make the lectures clear, interesting and acceptable. One could look at the eyes of the students—sometimes gleaming and sometimes dull—and realise whether one was going on the right track. There was no personal contact with the majority of the students. They were merely faces and roll numbers, but in the mass they represented what a writer would regard as his reading public or a musician as his audience.

It is no use denying that there is sometimes a histrionic element in teaching, but it has to be subdued. The important thing is that a teacher in a big class has to catch the mood of his students and then to shape it in a sympathetic direction.

The Honours classes were small and I had in these classes some brilliant students whom it was a pleasure to teach. With them I could develop close personal contact. They were welcome at any time in my bachelor's room nearby. This personal contact—a practice I retained till the end of my days as a teacher—probably benefited the students, but it benefited me more, because I could see where their difficulties lay and what would require detailed explanation in the class lectures.

Some of my Honours students at Ripon College rose to high positions in academic life and in the administrative services later. I meet them even now and reminisce with pleasure about the salad days when the students were just entering adult life and when I was expanding my experience. I made mistakes and even blunders, but the lessons were learnt and my students remember only the pleasures of our association.

The major part of my lecture-hours was devoted to the Intermediate students with whom Civics (with Economics) was a very popular subject. In the crowded classes, there always were a score or so of very bright students sitting around the teacher and taking in every word. This compelled the teacher to be very careful in his presentation. The best among the Intermediate students did not all take up Economics at the B.A. stage and even when they did they quite justifiably moved over to Presidency College. But the contacts that were developed remained. I meet many of those students now with pride—university professors in English, or Comparative Literature, or History or Economics, college teachers, top-level bank officers, flourishing advocates and high court judges.

I have been somewhat expansive about Ripon College because it was this college that set me firmly on my growth as a teacher. It gave me experience and it gave me confidence in myself. After eight years at Ripon College, I was ready for anything—large classes and small classes, bright students and indifferent ones. If there was an appropriate technique or mix of techniques required in teaching different types of students under different conditions, Ripon College gave me the right lessons. I owe a deep debt of gratitude to my students at Ripon College who built me up as a teacher in my formative years between the ages of twenty-four and thirty-two. And there were my colleagues who helped me to become much more developed as an individual than I was when I entered the college.

I left Ripon College in 1943 with a wrench in my heart. I knew that the government would not put me at Presidency College right from the start but I could not disregard the pay, time-scale, promotion prospects, pension benefits and everything else that were then available only in government service.

The college at which I was placed was established in the nineteen-twenties for Muslim students. Non-Muslims were not barred, but practically no one came. The founders of the college could not anticipate that the best among the Muslim students even would not

The Adventure of Teaching

come to this college, in preference to Presidency or the good Missionary colleges. After Ripon College, the classes appeared very small and rather sleepy. One could not be sure that there would be even a single student in the Economics Honours class every year. But still, my five years at Islamia College marked a further step in my own education.

I had to face a different set of teaching conditions and had to be careful that I did not tread on any political corn. The students were extremely polite and helpful. I gratefully remember the courage with which they protected their non-Muslim teachers during the great Calcutta communal riots of 1946. The college was located at a very sensitive place and the students always escorted us across the troubled area. One of the leaders of the students was a young man named Sheikh Mujibur Rahman, but no one could then guess that here was the creator of the sovereign state of Bangladesh.

III

And then I came to Presidency College after two years' study leave abroad and taught there for the rest of my teaching career. While still at Ripon College and later at Islamia, I had started teaching in the postgraduate classes of the University as a part-time lecturer and that had already brought me in touch with the best among the students of Bengal. The postgraduate classes were sometimes as large as those at Ripon College and there was a noisy road just below the classrooms here also. But there were students whom it was a pleasure to talk to. They had already taken their B.A. Honours degree in Economics —the best ones mainly from Presidency College with some from Scottish Church. Three of my students of that period became vice-chancellors and many became university professors, high-court judges, top administrators and high officers in international bodies. I remember gratefully the hard questions they sometimes asked, making me think deeply and read extensively, so that I would not disappoint them. I received from them a stimulus that was very valuable at that stage.

Such stimulus I received in a much larger dose at Presidency College. The Economics Department of the college had always been remarkably brilliant and it was generally accepted that all the first-class places in the Honours list would be won by its students. If there was any exception in any year, there was considerable heart-search-ing both among teachers and students. When I entered the Department as a teacher in 1950, I found that the eighteen years that had lapsed between my student days and my entry as a teacher had suddenly rolled themselves away and I felt that I was back home again. The years I spent at the college were years of remarkable efflorescence of young talent. I had then had some experience of how this explosion was being translated into effective teaching in universities abroad.

At Presidency I got finely-attuned responsive students whom I could attempt to shape from their first year undergraduate class and carry the attempt on up till their final year M.A. These students have now become world-famous economists and they are to be found everywhere—in governmental policy-making bodies and in universities, in India and abroad. It is not necessary for me to name them, for their names are at every economist's finger-tips. I may only quote what I said in March 1984 at the Bengal Economic Conference: "I do not know if I will live long enough to see one of my students win the Nobel Prize, but I do know that some of them have done work of a quality far superior to that of some of the winners of the award."

We who had been teachers of Economics at Presidency College in the fifties have often in the public eye shared in the glory reflected from our outstanding students. Perhaps we did something for them, but the important historical fact was that Economics was then becoming a challenging subject all over the world and Presidency College shared in the development. Among our students here Economics was a magnet that attracted the keenest of the minds, the only competing choice being theoretical Physics. The IIT's were coming up, but they were yet to become the strong attractive force. We could be sure that we would get 30 or 40 of the best students of the university. At that historically opportune period, I had the opportunity of being at the crucial location. Our students may have been attracted by us, but they could not escape us either.

In the great adventure of teaching at Presidency College, I had the good fortune of having outstanding team-mates. There was our Senior, Professor Upendranath Ghosal, whose lucid exposition of the subject (which then included Political Science also) was incomparable. Tapas Majumdar was a fresh addition to the faculty immediately after taking his Master's degree and he enriched the Department with his cultivated and fertile mind and incisive analytical powers

And then gradually the department expanded and others started coming—our own recent students returning as feedbacks to their own department. Some came for short periods and some came to stay. Among them were Dhires Bhattacharya, Nabendu Sen, Sukhamoy Chakravarti, Amiya Bagchi, Mihir Rakshit, Bimal Jalan and many others. The only one who was not an old student of the department was Dipak Banerjee, who had taken a degree in Chemistry from Presidency and then had gone to the London School of Economics to get a B.Sc. Econ. with an unbroken set of A grades. Banerjee and Rakshit are valiantly keeping up the old traditions of the department amidst the emerging unhelpful and even inimical forces.

In my time, however, there was a marked improvement in the infrastructural facilities and the government authorities were really helpful. We were given a whole block of rooms in the newly-constructed extension of the science laboratories in the place of one dark room in the main building. Every teacher got a cubicle for himself fitted in such a way that he could hold his tutorial classes there. We brought the books on Economics from the main library to our departmental library which give much better reading and loaning facilities. We got our separate library and office staff. With a larger faculty and more accommodation, we could introduce innovations like one-student tutorials.

There were other innovations to which the students responded heartily. We did not then care much about the syllabus and textbooks prescribed by the university—we knew our students would do well at the examinations—and proceeded along lines devised by ourselves. I tried a number of experiments.

For example, once I used a whole month of about eight or nine lectures in explaining the tools of analysis before plunging into the subject matter. On two or three occasions, I gave my first year students a few lectures on the history of economic thought, so that they might not have any difficulty if later they got a reference to the physiocrats or the classicals. Against stiff opposition, we made Mathematics a compulsory subsidiary subject for the Economics Honours students in our college. The university adopted this rule much later. We took charge of the college examinations for our students and told them that there would be no invigilation, though the teacher in charge would remain in his room all the time and there would be a bearer to help the students by supplying extra paper etc. We found that our trust in the students was not misplaced, but there was serious objection from other departments.

There was one important lesson that I learnt at Presidency College. A teacher no doubt has to carry his students through a process of exposition. This is imperative, but it is more important to create a love for the subject, a love which will impel the students to go further afield. With highly capable students in the class, one could feel sure that they could easily learn the subject from the excellent books that were then coming out. They did not require any spoon feeding or any waste of time over details when the fundamental logic was clear. If the teacher can enliven the students' curiosity and spirit, he succeeds in his task.

A second important lesson I learnt was that a teacher can command respect only if he is intellectually honest, never shirking a difficult problem and never failing to confess openly that he cannot always give a full explanation of a question without further study and thinking. I felt that I could easily admit my limitations and this helped me in securing appreciation for what I could actually do for them.

I have already mentioned the importance of personal contact outside the classrooms. This is easier in a residential university than in a metropolitan institution. But the classes at Presidency College were small—around 40 when there was a two-year combined Honours course in Economics and Political Science and, later, around 25 when the two subjects were separated in the three-year system. It was possible to know every student even inside the classroom, but they came to our rooms and to our homes whenever they liked.

This was a major difference between my student days at Presidency College and my days as a teacher twenty years later. As students we were not allowed to enter the Senior Common Room (most of the teachers did not have individual rooms for themselves) and had to send in a slip seeking an interview. There was not much of an interview, for the teacher, if he was in, would come out to the veranda and try to return to his sanctum as quickly as possible. There were innumerable funny stories about teachers mixing up their students.

We changed all that and our gain was probably more than that of the students. These contacts lasted beyond the allotted years and were in many cases never broken. The old students still come to me, sometimes with copies of their new books or papers and sometimes for a purely social visit. At one time, I taught them; now they write and talk and I learn. They are my teachers now. I have probably ceased to grow as a teacher, but I am still growing as a student.

IV

I left my regular appointment at Presidency College in 1962. I could have stayed for another six years, but I was persuaded to accept an administrative appointment in the Education Department. My social conscience was not hurt as I was leaving the Department in highly capable hands and the loss was entirely mine. When I finally retired in early 1969 after four years and a half in educational administration and a year and a half on the Finance Commission, I renewed my association with the college. By that time my successors had taken the department to higher stages of development, the most important being the establishment of a research center with aid from the University Grants Commission.

The department had in the past concentrated more on teaching than on research and the only sponsored research in my time was one assisted by the Research Programmes Committee of the Planning Commission. But my successors built up an excellent research unit, some of the products of which—like the study of steel production in India—have been widely acclaimed as first-rate. There had, of course, always been individual research by the members of the faculty—both doctoral and post-doctoral. Some of the books based on such research have become classics.

The Government of West Bengal (persuaded by my former colleagues) did me the honour of appointing me an Emeritus Professor in the department. This was an honour I greatly valued. Naturally, there were no fixed rights or obligations, but in the first few years after my retirement, I used to go to all the seminars arranged at the college and also gave a few special courses of lectures on extra-curricular subjects.

I still find that I am back to my younger days when I am in front of a blackboard, with pieces of chalk in my hand, facing the same type of expectation and appreciation that was my good fortune to get years ago. I also feel that I am still growing when I am invited to give endowment or special lectures at universities, or a course of lectures at 'house' institutions like the training colleges for bankers. I attend seminars—there are many of them now—and while I participate in the discussion when I can, I enjoy listening to what the others say. That way I keep in touch with the thinking of the new generation.

Teaching is a great adventure with its own romance and thrill. But sometimes it is great fun also. I still remember the ultra-serious student at Burdwan who wrote inordinately long answers to the examination questions. When I asked him to write more relevantly, he said that he had reproduced the whole chapter in which the matter was discussed and the relevant answer must be somewhere there. It was evidently my function to find it out.

I once found a young man at the back of the room furiously writing without raising his head even to look at the diagram I had drawn on the blackboard. I caught him at the end of the period and he said that he was not a student of the class at all, but was training himself as a stenographer. He found my class the best place for practising his shorthand—a compliment I did not quite appreciate.

Students think they know very well the mannerisms of their teachers. In fact, in a social function on one occasion, a student (he is a top administrator now) gave caricatures of all his teachers. I was one of his subjects and I found that I was not at all conscious of my mannerisms—both physical and verbal.

What the students do not perhaps realise is that the perceptive teacher also knows something about his students' mannerisms. There are some whose eyes light up when they feel that an idea is opening up. There are others who take notes patiently, sometimes looking lost when a particular word or expression has not registered. There are a few who look straight at you all through the hour, making you feel that something must be wrong with the knot of your neck-tie. And then there are those who nod in appreciation. Some nod intermittently, probably encouraging you to go ahead and there are some who nod continuously, making it difficult for you to understand what their real feelings are, or whether this is a case simply of the Pavlov reflex.

Such a 'nodder' once placed me in great confusion. I believe everyone has read Wodehouses's story of the Nodders, where the Chief Nodder, assisted by Vice-nodders and Deputy-nodders nodded dutifully when the Hollywood tycoon employing them would make a

The Adventure of Teaching

suggestion. This student (in one of my large post-graduate classes where I did not know all of them) seemed to nod violently in protest against everything I said, but he did not say anything. The next day I saw his name in the register and found that he came from South India. That explained the mystery, for, as everyone knows, the South Indians have their own style of rotating their heads. When they mean to say 'Yes' with a movement of their heads, they seem to the Northerners to be saying 'No'.

It will be unkind to list the students' howlers I had come across, particularly when I know of absurd howlers committed by reputed teachers. But some were pure art. I cannot forget the student who, after explaining Malthus' theory of population, stated that this theory was replaced by a more scientific one developed by Professor Optimum. There was the student (in the days when Marshall had to be read), who wrote "Rent is the leading species of a large *genius*", or the one who quite justifiably used the word 'inflammation' for 'inflation'. And there were some delightful Spoonerisms like Robin Joanson for Joan Robinson.

An interesting feature of my times was the evolution of co-education—from a trickle of women students to a torrent. In my student days, we were a little envious of Scottish Churches College (now simply Scottish Church), which admitted women students. There were women students at the university, but very few had the inclination to come to Economics. As a teacher, I had a lone girl student at Burdwan, but there were none at Ripon or Islamia. There were always a few in the postgraduate classes when I started teaching there. At first the practice was for the teacher to go to the girls' common room and escort them to the class, and then at the end of the period, to shepherd them back to their safe haven. Gradually, the system changed to one in which the girls waited outside the classroom entering and leaving with the teacher. And still later it became common to find them already seated in the classroom.

As the number of girl students increased, further changes took place. The ultimate in this was reached in English Honours at Presidency College where there were once 18 girls and 2 boys in the class. The girls kept the room in their occupation. The boys waited outside and entered the class with the teacher. This was co-education with a vengeance. In many subjects like literature (English, Bengali or

Sanskrit), or philosophy, the girl students now dominate. Apart from lending a grace and decorum to the ambience, they impress the teacher by their seriousness in studies.

They have fewer diversions than the boys and are painstakingly thorough in everything. This thoroughness is sometimes overdone. There was a young lady who would take down everything including, of course, the diagrams drawn by me on the blackboard. I once put a tick-mark in the figure to emphasise a point. That tick-mark duly reappeared in the answer-script at the next examination. On the whole, the performance of the girl students is of a very high order. I remember one year in which all the top places in the M.A. examination in Economics were taken by them.

I ought to record the fact that in general I had no trouble with the authorities and my personal academic freedom was almost absolute. There was a minor incident in my very young days as a teacher, when the vice-principal of the college complained that I went a little too fast in my lectures. I told him that I planned my lectures after taking into account the scheduled holidays also and I had to pack in more per lecture than I had planned because of the unscheduled holidays he himself often declared. That was the end of the matter.

The only major incident was one in which M.A. candidates left the examination hall (led or forced only by a few) complaining against the question paper I had set. They did not say that the questions were stiff; their argument was that they did not get the questions they had expected from what the teacher of the subject had led them to believe. The university decided to give grace marks to the students on the basis of their marks in other papers. I protested and suggested that the students should be examined again on a question paper set by any reputed external examiner. The authorities chose the path of the least resistance and awarded liberal grace marks. I resigned and since then have not participated in postgraduate teaching and examinations. It was much later that the authorities started taking a strong position against examination malpractices and disruptions. My informal touch with the postgraduate department has of course remained unaffected.

Memories throng themselves into an old man's mind. Often in the 'stilly night', when Calcutta is having its usual long power cuts and I am reclining on an easy chair waiting for the lights to dispel the solid darkness, it is the light of other days that illuminates my mind. I go back, as if in a dream, to the undulating campus at Chittagong, the dark and sombre classrooms at Burdwan, the crowded classes, corridors and staircases at Ripon College, the kind atmosphere at Islamia and the intellectually exciting days at Presidency and the University.

All this shaped me as a teacher and made me proud of being one. In the real world of inflation-induced erosion of income and the unrelenting struggle against the shortages of the minimum essentials of life, these memories—memories that are all smiles and no tears—keep me alive. Living on memories alone is a cessation of growth, but I wake up from my dreams and start thinking about the next day's seminar or lecture engagement. The process of growth continues, though perhaps at a slow rate.

V

Does the life-time experience of an individual yield a philosophy—one that goes beyond the individual and is relevant to all who belong to his set? It is necessary to be cautious against the temptation to overstate one's presumptions. Teaching is often described as a sacred mission, but there is a 'mission' element in practically all professions—particularly of doctors, rural welfare workers and local administrators.

In the past, the missionary aspect of teaching was often emphasised to find a social justification for paying the teachers low wages. It is only recently that the need for providing the teachers with the minimum resources for decent living has been recognised. On the other hand, it is a mistake to think that there is a positive relation between good salaries and good teaching. While society owes the teachers their legitimate dues and has to maintain teaching as an attractive choice for young intellects, the teachers have to ask themselves the question whether they are doing what society expects from them.

The question of social responsibility requires careful scrutiny. As in the case of the 'mission' aspect, social responsibility is an important element in the work of the doctor, engineer or administrator. This responsibility is different from accountability, for the former is a moral obligation, while the latter is a legal one. It is easy to satisfy the obligation of accountability—whether to the concerned group, or to the auditors and monitors, or to the legislature.

It is much more difficult to satisfy the moral obligation of social responsibility. In this, the teacher is in a very special position. The direct recipients of his services are very young persons who do not often know what exactly they are entitled to. If a teacher takes his duties lightly, there may be students who will not mind at all. Every teacher has the experience of the inordinate delight among the students, when a teacher is absent or when there is an unscheduled cessation of the daily work-period.

There is the possibility that a really serious teacher goes unappreciated—particularly if he is placed in a college which does not choose its students carefully. There is the more common opposite possibility—of a superficial but flashy teacher, with a gift of the tongue, impressing his students more by the flow of his words than by the contents of his lecture. Very few teachers can leave a permanent impression on his students and that makes the creation of an alluring but fleeting impression appear as success.

In about every profession, the direct 'customers' are adults with a clear idea of what they want. A doctor cannot easily deceive his patients, but a teacher can mislead his students into thinking that they are getting the right service.

And, then, there are teachers who care little for their mission and social responsibility but become as commercial as any trader. There are occasional reports about outright corruption, in admitting students and in seeing them through their examinations. Such cases are fortunately rare, but the moral aspect of coaching classes and the like has not been fully evaluated by our society. Even a teacher who gets a good salary cannot sometimes be indifferent to the prospect of earning large sums through private coaching, or by writing cram books.

The incomes earned by such methods remain 'undeclared' and are therefore effectively tax-free. There is no legal or ethical difference between the black income of the traders in essential goods and the off-white incomes of those who trade in what is believed to be education. Again, it is to be emphasised that such educational traders are not many in number. The large majority of teachers do their best, for otherwise the whole system would have crumbled.

There is no easy way in which a sense of social responsibility and moral rectitude can be forced on a teacher. All brave attempts at meaningful evaluation have up till now ended in a whimper. Teachers' promotions to higher scales do not depend these days on merit alone. The personal promotion scheme (with its attendant abuses), the rules for 'stagnation promotion' and trade union pressure have all combined to make the total length of service the only important factor. And 'merit' again is very difficult to judge.

Some of the persons who are very highly qualified in terms of degrees and even published papers are poor teachers. The routine emphasis given by the selection bodies to research degrees has turned the doctorate into a racket, on which chapters can be written.

A final point has to be made about the conduct of the teacher in his academic life. It is not necessary that the teacher should be a model to his student in every respect, but he should not be a bad example. When teachers are seen openly adopting methods which are considered normal only in industrial establishments, one cannot blame the students if they show indiscipline and disorder.

One hears often that when there is student trouble in a college or university, there are teachers to instigate them. There is no reason why the teacher should not fight for a right cause, but it is necessary to be circumspect about what is right and it is also essential to remember that young students will in their own behaviour emulate what they see their teachers doing. It is short-sighted not to realise that such emulation may recoil on the teachers themselves.

Ultimately, one has to fall back on the conscience of the teacher and on his own perception of job-satisfaction. Small classes, a good teacher-student ratio, good libraries, laboratories and other infrastructural facilities all help and a good tradition, once built up, creates its own momentum. But conscience cannot be manufactured and the artist's pleasure in a job well done is not everyone's dream.

Good teachers are not born and they are not made either. They have to make themselves good by their own effort. Such effort is largely individual, but partly collective also, for when an individual falters, the group of which he is a part can instil in him the required enthusiasm. Groups which act in unison for maintaining and raising the standards and for making education socially meaningful do exist and it is on their will and strength that we ultimately depend for the growth of skill, intellect and culture.

3
A Career in a Declining Profession

ANDRE BETEILLE

I became a university teacher at the age of twenty-four and have been one ever since, remaining in the same institution in which I began my career in the academic profession more than twenty-five years ago. I think of this institution in various ways: sometimes as the Department of Sociology and at others as the University of Delhi, but perhaps most often as the Delhi School of Economics. I have taught— or lectured—in various other institutions both in India and abroad, but have never been more than a visitor in any one of them.

When I look back on my early days as a university teacher what strikes me is not simply that I myself was young then but that the institution which I joined was also young. I came to a brand new department, for it was set up in 1959, the year in which I joined it. The Delhi School of Economics had moved into its new building a couple of years earlier, having spent the first few years of its life in the recesses of the Arts Faculty building. The University of Delhi was itself new, at least as an institution of postgraduate study and research. Its first two professors were appointed in 1942, Professor V.K.R.V. Rao and Professor D.S. Kothari and they were both in the university when I joined it, the former as its Vice-Chancellor and the latter as the head of its Department of Physics.

The place to which I came in 1959 was not only new, it was at the same time both small and spacious. I find it difficult to describe the sense of space I felt when I first came to live and work in the University of Delhi. I had come from Calcutta where the university was crowded and cramped. There was no campus in Calcutta. The buildings were in different parts of the city, mostly in crowded areas. There were no staff quarters and hardly any gardens. The Delhi

A Career in a Declining Profession

School of Economics had then a single building which looked imposing even though its architectural merit was slight.

It stood on its own grounds where both trees and flower beds were well maintained. The whole was enclosed by a wall which had three gates of which the tallest was always kept shut. I was told that these gates were designed after some college in Cambridge, and it was not too difficult in those days to maintain the illusion that one was in Cambridge or some equally enchanted seat of learning. The Delhi School of Economics was a privileged place, and I counted myself lucky to have got a lecturership there at the very beginning of my academic career. Others were to become professors in the same institution while still in their twenties.

The sense of space was enhanced by the smallness of numbers. One did not have to contend with crowds in the Delhi School of Economics or, for that matter, anywhere in the University of Delhi. The Department of Sociology was very small. Until it became a Centre of Advanced Study in 1968, it had half-a-dozen teachers, a dozen or so research students and around fifteen students in each of the two M.A. classes. The Department of Economics was larger, with more teachers and more students, but in the early years lectures for M.A. students in Economics were held elsewhere, and only those on the rolls of the Delhi School of Economics—about forty in each of the two M.A. classes—had tutorials in the School.

Because the place was spacious and the numbers were small, teachers were given individual rooms. I shared a room with two other lecturers in the department for a while, but within a couple of years I had my own room. I valued that room above most things, and without it the pattern of my academic life might have been very different. Indian academics cannot afford spacious homes, particularly when they are young, and it is difficult to do sustained academic work without security against intrusion. Teachers in Indian universities, especially in the humanities, do not generally have individual rooms, and their habits of work cannot be understood without taking that fact into account.

II

The Delhi School of Economics was not only a privileged place, it was also a place of academic distinction. The Department of Sociology was headed by M.N. Srinivas who combined great academic distinction with enormous personal charm. I will not talk about his contribution to sociology which is widely acknowledged. What is more important is the sense he conveyed to each one of us of the value of sociology and of the dignity of the academic profession. The Department of Economics, as I said, was larger, having had an earlier start. In the sixties it had a great accession of strength, becoming easily the best Department of Economics in the country and, for its size, one of the best in the world. It was in the sixties that the two Departments, first of Economics and then of Sociology, became Centres of Advanced Study.

A change came about in the atmosphere of the Delhi School of Economics in the sixties, beginning in the Department of Economics. When I came to the School, Professor Srinivas was the Head of the Department of Sociology and Professor B.N. Ganguli of the Department of Economics. Professor Ganguli was also the Director of the School. They were both men of great dignity who commanded respect as much by their professional standing as by their scholarly attainments. Professor Ganguli was in every respect the seniormost member of the institution. We used to all have tea in the afternoons in the staff room, and when he walked in as he occasionally did, we all stood up.

Professor Srinivas had a proper sense of institutional hierarchy. He deplored the excesses of both traditionalism and modernism. He had great contempt for what he called 'the north Indian habit of feet-grabbing', i.e., the custom—presumably more widely observed in the North than in the South—whereby junior academics greet their seniors in both private and public places by touching their feet. But he also considered distasteful the back-slapping social style common in American academic circles. He was a Tamil Brahmin who had been an Oxford don.

The appointment in the sixties of a number of very young and very outstanding professors in the Department of Economics undermined the correspondence between academic attainment and professional seniority on which every institutional hierarchy rests. Some were dismayed by the fact that one of the new professors was not only in his twenties but did not have either a book or a Ph.D. degree, although his later achievements fully vindicated his appointment. The hierarchical spirit was replaced by a competitive one, although this did not immediately affect my own department. I spent most of my time with my students and colleagues in Sociology, although I was personally well acquainted with the new professors in the other department. They were clearly playing in a different league and took little trouble to conceal that fact from their friends and colleagues.

III

Personally, I find an intensely competitive academic environment oppressive. It tends to turn one's mind to quick results and short cuts, and in the end to undermine what is of supreme value to scholarship, namely, the disinterested pursuit of the truth. At the same time, a competitive academic system has an advantage over an hierarchical one. It keeps up a certain pitch of activity and does not allow people to rest on their oars. There was a high pitch of intellectual activity in the Delhi School of Economics in the sixties, and it attracted people from all over the country and from many parts of the world. This intellectual traffic was not without its distractions but it was also exhilarating, particularly for students who were able to feel that they were in the centre of things or at least not very far from it.

Along with the competitiveness and the pitch of intellectual activity went a certain disregard for distinctions of rank. (I must insist that the disregard for distinctions of rank is healthy in an academic institution only when intellectual activity is at a high pitch, otherwise it degenerates into surliness and disorder.) When I first came to the university most departments had a single professor who was also the head; he was usually a patriarch and often a despot. I lived in those days in a university hall of residence along with a dozen other lecturers from various departments who told me the most hair-raising stories about what they were required to do for their professors. The Delhi School of Economics was far away from all this. It did not by any means do away with all distinctions, but academic distinction did not entitle anyone to push others around.

There was a self-consciously virtuous denigration of administrative office and rank, a kind of 'more-academic-than-thou' attitude among the professors. To be head of the department or even Director of the Delhi School of Economics came to be regarded as a nuisance and a bore. This had its good side but it also led in the long run to a certain devaluation of the institution itself. Even today any professor who is anyone in the Delhi School of Economics tends to look down upon administrative office—unless it is some very superior office in the government.

It was in the Delhi School of Economics that the principle of rotation first gained acceptance. In 1962 Professor Ganguli left the School to become the first Pro-Vice-Chancellor of the University, and Professor K.N. Raj succeeded him as both Director of the Delhi School of Economics and head of the Department of Economics. He was a great enthusiast for the principle of rotation and immediately set about applying that principle to the office of the Director.

A few years later it was extended to the headship of the Department of Economics, and when Professor Raj became Vice-Chancellor for a brief period in 1969-70, steps were taken to introduce the principle of rotation in all the departments of the university. The principle of rotation has altered the character of the university department, having had consequences which were not all foreseen by its early enthusiasts. It can work successfully only where there is some commitment to liberal democratic values, and that commitment cannot be created overnight.

As a young lecturer, I benefited greatly from the liberal atmosphere of the Delhi School of Economics. Much of that atmosphere still survives, despite the turmoil through which the university has passed in recent years. Distinctions of rank do not count for very much in the functional division of labour. In my own department, professors, readers and lecturers all do much the same kind of work and participate on an equal footing in the decision-making process. Every permanent teacher, irrespective of rank, has a room to himself, and the rooms are all of the same size and all furnished in the same way.

Physically, great changes have taken place in the Delhi School of Economics, as in the rest of the university in the last twenty years. Although many plans were made, things did not work according to plan. The university as a whole has expanded enormously. There are now both many more students and many more teachers. In the Delhi School of Economics the open spaces have been taken up by several new buildings, generally mean-looking. The departments have become separated from each other, at least physically and the place has become crowded. The shine has gone out of the institution although it still retains the academic ethos that was built up in the fifties and sixties.

In the fifties and sixties, when the Delhi School of Economics was acquiring its character as a premier academic institution, the older universities in Calcutta, Madras, Allahabad and, to some extent, Bombay, were becoming more and more provincial. The four of us who made up the faculty of the Department of Sociology in 1959 all came from different parts of the country, and the faculty of the Delhi School of Economics has always had an all-India character. Unlike most other institutions in India, we continue to attract students from all parts of the country. This is an index as well as a source of the continued academic vitality of the Delhi School of Economics.

IV

The Delhi School of Economics established high standards of teaching and research, and has been on the whole successful in maintaining those standards, despite the rising pressure of numbers and despite the loss of some of its more talented teachers. Certain material conditions are necessary for creating and maintaining a proper atmosphere for teaching: adequate classrooms for students, individual rooms for teachers, clean toilets for everyone, and a well-stocked library. But a great deal can be done on modest resources through the initiative and imagination of a small number of dedicated teachers. The Delhi School of Economics was fortunate in having such teachers in its early days, and the habits of work created by them still survive to a large extent.

University teachers are not assigned work schedules in the way in which office or factory workers are. They have considerable autonomy in arranging their own programmes of work. This is not wholly free from disadvantage. In the absence of a well-established work ethic, autonomy is turned into licence, and teachers satisfy themselves by meeting only the formal requirements of teaching which are not, as in the case of school teachers, very heavy. It is not, however, only a question of work ethic.

Where the physical basis of regular and sustained work is lacking, teachers can easily slip into apathy and negligence. What I have in mind may be illustrated by contrasting the work habits of teachers in science and arts departments. Science teachers are obliged to work within the discipline of the laboratory for which there is no exact counterpart in the case of arts teachers. As a result, the latter tend to be more lax and irregular in their work than the former.

A room for one's own use is a great asset in this context. I use my room in the Department of Sociology not only for reading and writing but also for meeting students and colleagues. A great deal of the time of a university teacher, particularly in the humanities, is spent in discussion, much of which is unfocussed or even aimless. The cumulative effect of this unfocussed discussion is substantial. It is through such discussion that one often picks up new facts, new ideas and new ways of looking at both. Formal supervision, whether of M.A. or Ph.D. students, takes place in this intellectual context.

V

Within my own academic career I have assigned more importance to teaching than to research, and the teaching of M.A. students has been at the centre of my work. Over the years we have developed in the Department of Sociology a pattern of teaching for M.A. students which I believe to be one of the best in the world. We are not always fortunate in the M.A. students we admit, but when we get a good batch, teaching reaches a very high standard of excellence. It rests on a combination of three components: (1) lectures, (2) seminars and (3) tutorials. I would like to briefly describe each of these in turn.

Lectures are delivered according to a time-table drawn up in advance for each semester. A set of lectures, usually three per week for the semester, is delivered for every course, and this is typically the responsibility of a single teacher. A teacher in the Department of Sociology does not usually carry a heavy lecture load. When I first started teaching I usually lectured on two courses at a time, but the lecture load of a young teacher today is a little lighter. Attendance at lectures was in the earlier days compulsory for students but it is now optional. While I believe that attendance at lectures should not be made compulsory for students, an advantage of the older system was that it discouraged irregularity among teachers.

Because I was never required to carry an excessive lecture load, I have been able to devote much time to the preparation of lectures. An important factor behind this in my case was the personal influence of M.N. Srinivas. He convinced me, by both argument and example, that a gift of the gab was usually a liability in a scholar. He was not himself a very eloquent speaker, and he never tired of telling me what a poor lecturer his teacher, Professor Evans-Pritchard, the great Oxford anthropologist, was. As is well known, Indians are among the most eloquent speakers in the world, and Indian academics often rely on their natural eloquence, neglecting to prepare their lectures. I do not regret my natural lack of eloquence for it has forced me to take great pains over the preparation of lectures.

VI

Both seminars and tutorials require more active participation by students and attendance at these, unlike at lectures, is compulsory. 'Participation' is a well-worn phrase among political theorists for some of whom it is a panacea for every evil. But any teacher who has struggled to engage his postgraduate students in active participation in serious academic work will know how difficult it is to keep them so engaged. Reading a seminar paper is a voluntary affair, and a student may have to be coaxed, cajoled and bullied into the task. Occasionally there are very willing students but these are not always the most able, and if the paper is very dull the class goes to sleep or many of its members quietly walk out. My experience of M.A. seminars is that students are inclined to be less kind to their fellow students than even to their teachers.

Seminar topics for a particular course are assigned by the teacher responsible for the lectures in that course. Usually three seminars are held for every course. Since there are sixteen courses in all, a total of 48 seminars are held which means that, in a class of about 50 students, each student ought to get a chance to read a seminar paper during the two years devoted to an M.A. class. It rarely works out quite as neatly as that, and participation in the seminar varies widely from one M.A. class to another. Despite variations and shortfalls, the seminar still serves a useful purpose in enabling the teacher to get to know his class and the students to know one another.

The tutorial organizes teacher-student interaction in small groups.

It has been a tradition in the Department of Sociology that *all* teachers, irrespective of rank, take part in the tutorial programme, and I made it a point to take my normal quota of tutorial classes even when, as head of the department, I carried extra administrative burdens for three years. For the purpose of tutorials the entire M.A. class of about 50 students is divided up into small groups which are assigned to the various teachers in the department who then act as tutors for their respective groups. Topics for tutorials are assigned by the teachers responsible for covering the various courses through lectures, and these are then taken by the various groups to their respective tutors. Apart from other things, the tutorial system exposes the student to at least two points of view on a particular subject, that of the person lecturing on it and that of the tutor.

There are two sides to the tutorial: discussion and writing. Most students in most Indian universities are not trained to do either. It requires some skill and great patience in a tutor to get students to discuss an academic topic in a serious way. They do not come prepared to a tutorial class, and generally expect the tutor to give a lecture on the topic for discussion. A successful tutor manages to get at least a few of the students in his charge to open up and express their views, but in order to do this one has to range across a wide variety of subjects and to spend an enormous amount of time. One is often tempted to give up the whole exercise and to finish the business with a short lecture on the assigned subject.

The average student is not taught to write an essay in either school or college. We may be eloquent and voluble in speech, but we lack balance and measure in writing. It is not easy to get a tutorial essay out of a student, but when he submits the essay it is usually three times the specified length. Our students write their answers at excessive length and then invariably complain that the question was lengthy. It is not easy to create a habit of writing clear and concise essays in M.A. students who are already in their twenties, and have their minds on many things besides their tutorials.

I have tried to explain the importance of combining lectures, seminars and tutorials in the teaching of M.A. students. I hope I have conveyed some sense of the difficulty of doing this effectively, for I do not believe that the difficulty is fully appreciated by people who make educational policy without being actively engaged in teaching.

Over the last 25 to 30 years the system has worked more or less satisfactorily in the Delhi School of Economics, especially in the Departments of Economics and Sociology. But it does not work for most other subjects in the University of Delhi at the postgraduate level, and I doubt if it is even tried out in a proper way in other universities in the country. Incidentally, I was told at the Erasmus University in Rotterdam, where I spent some time as a visitor, that they did not have such a system as it would be too costly.

VII

Apart from M.A. students, I have of course also had research students. Research students include both M. Phil. and Ph. D. students, but for want of space I shall confine the discussion to only the latter. It is difficult to devise standard procedures for the instruction of Ph.D. students, given the enormous variation in their abilities, aptitudes and interests. There is of course the research seminar which has a somewhat different format from that of the M.A. seminar. The research seminar can be quite useful to the Ph.D. student since it enables him to see how ideas take shape through the interaction of minds. But it can also be quite intimidating to the neophyte if he happens to get caught in a crossfire between academic heavyweights.

I have been somewhat handicapped in my academic career by the fact that I find seminars rather boring. I have not attended many seminars outside India, so I will speak only of those I have attended in our country. Indian academics are not only very voluble, they are also supremely status conscious. At a seminar they often intervene not because they have something to say but because they feel that their academic standing makes silence inappropriate. Much depends on how seminars are conducted, and when they are well conducted, they can be an educative experience. I still recall vividly the time when the research seminar in the department was conducted by M.N. Srinivas. He was a superb seminar chairman who never dominated the discussion and made everyone feel that he might have something important to say.

Whatever may be the value of the research seminar, it cannot replace individual supervision of the student by the teacher. Here much depends on the personal equation between the two. I have never had a research student with whom my relationship did not at some point become strained, either because I felt that he was not doing enough work or because he felt that I was applying undue pressure.

Managing a relationship with a Ph.D. student is not easy. Not only is he an adult person with his own convictions and his own sense of dignity, but there is always some area of enquiry in which his knowledge is, or ought to be, superior to his supervisor's. A Ph.D. student cannot be treated on exactly the same footing as an M.A. student; he has to be given a longer rope.

VIII

I believe it was a mistake on the part of the University Grants Commission at one stage to make a research degree a necessary qualification for all college teachers. Research calls for a very special kind of intellectual temper, and the research degree ought not to be devalued. For undergraduate teaching a habit of extensive reading is far more useful than research on a specialized topic. It is true that knowledge becomes very rapidly outdated in the modern world, but the remedy for that is to provide undergraduate teachers with general facilities for keeping abreast of the literature, not to impose a uniform requirement that every teacher should secure a Ph.D. degree. This is not to say that a college teacher who is inclined to work for a research degree should not be encouraged to do so.

Research calls for a certain independence of mind, a quality which was never actively fostered in our traditional cultural environment. In a social world in which a young man expects his elders to find a wife and an occupation for him, one should not expect too much initiative in the pursuit of ideas. The majority of research students expect their supervisors to find suitable topics for them and suitable ways of dealing with them. There are, however, many exceptions in the Delhi School of Economics which is able to attract the best students in the country. I have myself had Ph.D. students who compare in sharpness of intelligence, though not in intellectual stamina, with the best I have known anywhere in the world.

The relationship between a supervisor and his research student is a difficult one because it has always a personal as well as an academic side. If a supervisor keeps too close a watch on his student, the student feels oppressed; if he is left wholly to himself, he feels rejected. My own students have on the whole felt rejected rather than oppressed because I have made it a practice not to intervene personally in securing a job for a person on the ground that he was my student. While I do not wish to make a virtue of my inability to promote my own students, I cannot fail to point to the relationship between that kind of promotion and academic factionalism.

IX

When I first started teaching I was not much older than my own students. A whole generation separates me from my present students. Many changes have taken place in the intervening years both in the institutional setting of academic life and in the orientation of the academic profession.

Students, teachers and *karamcharis* have increased at an exponential rate. Not only have numbers greatly increased, the increase has been rapid, unplanned and under pressure. The massive increase in numbers has brought about qualitative changes in the relations between people. Teachers who have been in the university for many years now feel that they have lost their grip over things.

When a university grows rapidly to a great size, academic life becomes difficult to manage on purely academic terms. The academic side of the University then inevitably loses out to the administrative and the political sides. This has happened in the University of Delhi, and it has been the general pattern in all universities throughout the country.

Twenty five years ago senior academics in the university, whether in the sciences or in the humanities, could hold their own if not with the Vice-Chancellor, then certainly with the Registrar. It is now quite common to find heads of departments waiting upon a Deputy Registrar or a Deputy Finance Officer. During the three years I served as head of the department I did not visit even once either the Registrar or the Finance Officer, but then my department probably suffered as a result.

The university administration has become a gigantic machine. When a teacher or a student applies for something, say study leave or extension of fellowship, he does not know at which end his application will come out. Notings are made on files by clerks, assistants, section officers and the rest on even the most trivial subjects. Everything is entangled in rules which are elaborate, unclear and mutually inconsistent. Nobody who is serious about teaching and research can hope to master those rules. Naturally, everybody wants to meet the Vice-Chancellor or the Pro-Vice-Chancellor or the Registrar or the Deputy Registrar to see if some way can be found of getting round the rules. Some way is almost always found of getting round them but through enormous waste of time and energy.

Everyone acknowledges that there are too many rules and that these are impediments to the smooth functioning of academic life. Committees are set up from time to time to streamline administrative procedures. These committees rarely take their work seriously and they recommend new rules and new procedures without ensuring that the old ones are discarded. The Indian approach to administration, in my view, is to create more and more rules, and to hope that some way will be found in the end to circumvent them. All this of course puts the academic at a disadvantage in relation to the administrator.

I do not wish to suggest that all professors are averse to administration. A life devoted solely to scholarship is extremely exacting and there are no assured rewards in it. Administration and committees provide escapes from the labours of research which must sometimes appear both endless and fruitless. Many academics shine on committees and, in a career of over a quarter century in the Delhi School of Economics, I have known several who have played important roles in planning and policy making. Most of these leave the university for good and only a few return to it, but those who return find it difficult to settle back into the dull routine of academic life.

The bureaucratization of academic life is a world-wide trend, but in a small postgraduate department of the kind in which I work no one can seriously complain that administrative responsibilities interfere substantially with academic work. Even as head of the department I did more or less the same amount of reading, writing and teaching that I ordinarily do. If one is serious about academic work it is better to be a victim of the administration than to join it in the hope of improving things.

X

What is time-consuming and exhausting is not academic administration but academic politics. Academic life has not only become more bureaucratized, it has become enormously more politicised. Although every teacher acquires some sense of this, its meaning became fully clear to me during the three years of my tenure as head of the department. Very broadly speaking, no major decision on any academic matter can now be taken solely on merit without consideration of the balance of power between students, teachers and *karamcharis*, and their various constituent parts.

The role of politics in academic life can be examined on two intersecting planes: firstly, on the plane of the department, faculty and the other constituent bodies of the university, and, secondly, on the plane of the unions of teachers, students and *karamcharis*.

Like bureaucratization, the democratization of universities has been a world-wide trend, but while academics are eloquent in denouncing the evils of the former, they rarely express any misgivings about the latter, even when they have them. I have found it extremely difficult to engage academics in a candid discussion of the political presuppositions and implications of the democratization of academic life.

Let me begin with an example of the positive side of democratization. When I joined the University of Delhi in 1959, the typical postgraduate department had a very hierarchical character. Barring a few exceptions, the department had a single professor who was also the head, and remained in that position till he retired. The head of the department had a decisive say on all matters pertaining to his department: appointments, admissions, scholarships, syllabus, time-table, etc. There was very little consultation within the department. There was enormous concentration of power in the hands of a single person and that person often acted as a despot.

All this has changed vastly with the introduction of the principle of rotation and with the growing influence of the Departmental Staff Council. There is more consultation now and the head can no longer act in a despotic manner. Older members of the university sometimes complain that democratization has robbed the departments of their coherence, and that loss of power has been accompanied by loss of interest among heads of departments. I believe that these are mostly problems of transition, and that from the purely academic point of view the new set-up is an advance over the old.

However, democratization is not a panacea for every evil, and I will now give an example of its negative side. The Academic Council is the supreme academic body of the University of Delhi. There has been a sea-change in its composition and character in the last twenty-five years. It has expanded greatly in size and has now a much larger component of elected teachers among its members.

It used to be a sedate and dignified body in which a small number of university professors and college principals played an active part. It is now a noisy, disorderly and totally unruly forum dominated by university officials on the one side and elected teachers on the other. I cannot in my entire professional career recall anything more disagreeable than the hours I have spent attending meetings of the Academic Council. There is nothing remotely academic in the atmosphere of those meetings.

Democracy in even a poor country need not take the form of populism, but the tragedy is that in what is called the 'teachers' movement' it invariably does. With the enormous growth in the size of the university, numbers have become more important than rank. It is true that in academic matters rank ought not to count for very much, but then numbers should count for even less. There is a story that when in the middle of World War II the German tanks were rolling into Russia, a well-meaning commissar suggested to Stalin that he might seek the support of the Pope. Stalin fixed him with a withering gaze, and asked, 'How many battalions does the Pope command?'

In the same spirit, those in authority now wish to satisfy themselves first about the support they may receive from the organized bodies of students, teachers and *karamcharis*. A Vice-Chancellor may ignore the advice of a Professor of Physics or a Professor of Economics, but he cannot treat lightly the views of the union leaders.

Industrial action by teachers has become an established practice in the University of Delhi. It enjoys the expressed or tacit support of virtually every section of the university, including ex-Vice-Chancellors if not Vice-Chancellors in office. A strike creates a sense of euphoria among college teachers; the arts professors try to divide the blame evenly between the union and the authorities; and the science professors try to get on with their work without making any noise.

The university authorities have to use all their wits to squeeze concessions from the government on the one hand, and, on the other, to keep at bay the rising demands of the union. The Vice-Chancellor begins by trying to keep everybody happy and ends by losing everybody's favour. The most striking effect of union activity in the University of Delhi may be seen in the physical appearance of the Vice-Chancellor's office which is now permanently enclosed in an iron cage.

XI

It is generally agreed that the University of Delhi, like most universities in the country, is passing through a difficult time. But there is difference of opinion about the principal causes behind the difficulty. Many people, including Vice-Chancellors, believe that university teachers work under conditions of great material hardship. It is true that they lack many of the amenities of middle-class life, but in a country where millions of people go without two meals a day, they cannot expect a rapid improvement in their material conditions to be made into a national priority. Others feel that there is too much interference by the government in the affairs of the university, and that the steady erosion of university autonomy is the most serious problem.

It is true that in some states ministers and civil servants have made universities their playthings, hiring and firing Vice-Chancellors at will, and treating university professors and college principals as members of their personal entourage. But it has not been quite like that in Delhi. There have been pinpricks from the University Grants Commission and, no doubt, from other official agencies, but the government has not tried seriously to interfere either with appointments or with admissions or with examinations in the University of Delhi.

Far more potent than government interference has been union action in the University of Delhi. Its potency is enhanced by the fact that while a hundred voices in the university will be raised—and rightly raised—against government interference, hardly anyone will speak openly against the coercive activities of the union. As the union has grown from strength to strength, its leaders have learnt to bypass the authorities in the colleges, the departments and the Faculties, and to negotiate directly with the Vice-Chancellor and the Executive Council. It may not be long before they bypass those as well and seek to negotiate directly with the Minister and his Secretary.

University professors will then bite their nails and hope that the government will behave responsibly. Nobody will behave responsibly if they abdicate responsibility. Academic autonomy is too precious a thing to be left in the care of either civil servants or trade unionists.

4
A Personal Narrative

J.N. KAPUR

I consider myself singularly fortunate in having been a teacher of generations of enthusiastic students in some of the best institutions in the world. I have been proud of my noble profession and if I were to be born again, I would once again like to be a teacher. My experience may therefore be of some value to those young men and women who aspire to be teachers or to those younger colleagues who are already in the profession.

I do not know when I started teaching, but I can certainly trace the beginnings of the adventure to my school days. As a class monitor, I had the responsibility of maintaining discipline in the classroom in the absence of the teacher. But I discharged this responsibility not by asserting my authority but by helping my class fellows, in the absence of the teacher as well as after the school was over. I was overwhelmed by the affection of my class fellows. They sometimes even welcomed the absence of the class teacher; now they could ask me to explain some lessons in an atmosphere of freedom.

My real initiation into teaching however came at the college stage. I had joined B.A. (Hons.) in Mathematics at Hindu College, Delhi. My head of the department was Prof. B.R. Seth, who had just returned from England after getting the prestigious D.Sc degree. By all standards, he was a brilliant mathematician. In his first lecture to our class of five students, he explained to us the basic principles of statics and said, "The rest of the course consists in the solution of problems. Start solving them and if you have any difficulties, bring these to the class." When we met next, he found that I had solved all the problems of the first set while no one else had been able to solve any problem at all. He asked me to do the problems on the blackboard. He was satisfied with my solutions as also with my way of explaining the problems.

From the next class onwards, the routine was that he would ask me if I needed the solution of any problem. If I replied in the affirmative, he would do so. After that he would walk out and leave the class in my charge. Subsequently even this formality was given up. I and four colleagues would sit down in whatever periods were free and I would remove their difficulties. My colleagues were happy because they could ask me all sorts of questions and raise all sorts of doubts which they dared not ask from Prof. Seth. We finished the course in half the time allotted for the purpose. I had a great motivation to study, to work hard and think clearly in order to satisfy my 'students'. Later the method of work was extended to other courses and the five of us formed a great team of students determined to learn on their own.

At the MA stage, I was the only student in the previous class. There were two students in the final year; one of them had actually finished his course but had decided not to appear in the university examination in order to improve his division. This time we three formed a group. My senior colleagues would explain to me the theory, even give the solutions of problems which they had solved and then ask me to solve more problems. Again it was an exciting one year of learning and teaching and in one year I had finished the two-year course completely.

In fact at the end of the first year my teachers decided that there was no point in setting papers for one student. One of my teachers was superintendent of university examinations. He asked me to sit in his room and gave me the university examination papers to solve along with other candidates. My papers were marked by my teachers and if I had been a regular candidate, I would have stood first in the university that year.

I had a whole year to revise my course, to teach these to new students and I knew almost everything to perfection. I got 97 per cent marks and beat the previous record by a wide margin of 15 per cent marks. I lost 16 marks in one question in one paper only and my teacher later told me, "You should have lost only 6 marks, but I deducted 16 marks, since I did not expect you to make that silly mistake."

My teachers had always high expectations of me and I always tried to rise up to their expectations. Later as a teacher, I had high expectations from my students and many of them rose to great heights in order not to disappoint me. This, in brief, is what teaching is about.

II

One great advantage which I had was my position as incharge of the departmental textbook library. I had all the important books under my charge. Whenever I failed to understand a point from one book, I went to another and if necessary to still another. I always found that the different points of view in different books helped to clarify the situation. However I had an overriding motivation to be absolutely clear myself for I had to explain the problems to my class-fellows, not by virtue of the authority of a teacher but by being absolutely clear and convincing.

I was fortunate in having great teachers, most of whom commanded great respect from their students. Teachers almost appeared as semi-gods and their examples provided great inspiration for the ideal of being a teacher. Unfortunately, the teaching profession has lost most of its glamour today. This is partly due to the steep rise in the number of students and teachers resulting in a large number of unmotivated teachers joining the profession and also because of the openings in a large number of professions which were not available when I was a student. However it is only the teachers who can rehabilitate the image of the teaching profession.

However I believe that there are still students in our colleges and universities who are attracted to the teaching profession. Let them start teaching even in their student days, let them teach their weaker class-fellows, let them teach junior students, let them teach students from weaker sections of society and let them get the thrill which comes from explaining and making things lucid and clear.

After my M.A. degree I got a teaching-cum-research assistantship in my college. I was not very much interested in research though I did present a paper at the Indian Science Congress. I threw myself wholeheartedly into the teaching programme. The seminar room which was my office was always full of students from all classes. Even students from other colleges used to come to my office and to my home. I had the reputation of being able to solve any problem in any text-book in any specialization in mathematics at a moment's notice. I acquired this reputation because I had worked out each of these problems dozens of times with different students.

Next year, in 1945, I joined Hindu College as a regular lecturer and since Prof. Seth was busy with his research and some family problems, I had to run the department almost single handed. Prof. Seth trusted me fully and his encouragement at every stage was a great asset.

During the summer of 1946, the first Indian Administrative Service Examination was held. My principal called me and urged me strongly to appear in the examination. I was most reluctant; I was enjoying my teaching work tremendously. He said, "Young man, you are bright, but you are a fool. Today you are getting the grade of Rs. 150-250, only two persons in the entire college get the grade of Rs. 300-500. I am sure after ten years you will get that grade and retire at age of 60 years at Rs 500 per month. As an IAS officer, you will have tremendous opportunities."

When I still refused, he attacked me at a weak point. "In you, we have an opportunity of beating St Stephen's College." I had sufficient loyalty to my college. I accepted the challenge. I prepared for a month, appeared in the examination, got the second position in all theory papers, but was pulled down to the seventh position in the interview. My principal was happy, but only for a short time.

I appeared in a hurried medical test. I reached there late. In fact I was out of breath after my bout of cycling. I was immediately called in and declared to be suffering from high blood pressure. During the last forty years, my blood pressure has been perfectly normal and many of the probationers who were declared fit then, later suffered from high blood pressure and other allied diseases.

I took this incident as God's confirmation of my decision to remain a teacher and I went about my work with great enthusiasm.

Another incident which failed to divert me from my path was the award of a Government of India scholarship to go to the USA for "River Research". The Government of India had decided in 1945 to send four to five hundred students for study abroad for the scientific and technological development of the country. Sir Maurice Gwyer, the then Vice-Chancellor of the University of Delhi was the chairman of the selection committee and the interviews were being held in his office. I got a call from his secretary to say that Sir Maurice Gwyer would like me to meet the selection committee. I went, was formally interviewed and was immediately selected on the basis of my academic record.

However some astrologers had told my mother that I should not cross the sea in a boat (there were no air flights in those days) and I decided to refuse the scholarship after the government had fixed trips on three different ships for me. The main reason was however not my mother's reluctance, but my lack of interest in river research as compared with the thrill which I got out of teaching.

III

In 1948, Prof. Seth went abroad and soon after coming back, he left to join the newly started IIT at Kharagpur as head of department of Mathematics. From the age of 25, I had worked as the de facto head of Mathematics department of a premier postgraduate college of the country.

The next ten years were the golden age of my teaching. The university statutes required a teacher to teach for 15-18 periods per week. I used to teach for 25-30 periods. Nobody asked me to do so. I did it because I enjoyed. Near the examination days, I used to take classes on Sundays. A class on Sunday would start at 11 AM and go on to 4 PM with a couple of 15 minutes tea breaks and in one day a whole paper would be revised. I did not do this so that my students might do better than students of other colleges. Students from other colleges were welcome to and in fact did attend my Sunday classes.

One interesting and inspiring experience of this period was the willingness of students to read courses not prescribed for the examinations. I had to teach a course in Statistics for three periods a week for one year. I told the students that I would teach six periods a week for two years and would teach them four times what was required for the examination. I invited only those students who were interested in going deep into the subject to offer this optional course. Seven students agreed and stuck till the end. Three of them later became distinguished professors of statistics; one became chairman of the Life Insurance Corporation, and one joined the IAS. These students were supposed to be "unwise" since they worked so hard for learning topics not needed for the examination. Ultimately they proved to be wiser than others.

For several years, I offered to teach new courses for which I got no credit for teaching and for which the students got no credit either. Every year I would find five or six students to audit such courses. I learnt a good deal of mathematics this way and both myself and the students enjoyed the experience. This also enabled us to introduce new courses in the university without any difficulty.

Another interesting experience was my representing the faculty members of the college on the Board of Governors of the college. The chairman was late Sir Shri Ram, the veteran industrialist. I had many clashes with him. Once when he said that the college had no funds to pay us the salaries immediately, I told him bluntly, "There are other persons who are willing to become the chairman and pay us the salaries, but we don't want it because we want to have an enlightened chairman like you. However please don't try our patience for long." He had developed great affection for me. He frowned for a moment and then relented and agreed to pay us our salaries within a week. I learnt a great deal from him and in spite of having differed with him strongly on several occasions, I developed great admiration for him.

I did not take part in sports or cultural activities in the college, but I acted as professor-in-charge of the college library, as bursar of the college and as joint secretary of the Old Students Association. However the assignment I liked most was the presidentship of the Students Helping Association. I started a textbook lending library for poor students and even organised some film shows for collecting funds for the same.

Those were great days for teaching. These were the first ten years after independence. There was great enthusiasm both among students and teachers. Students had respect for their teachers and teachers had love for their students. There were no strikes, no copying, no cutting of classes either by students or teachers. There was no eve-teasing, no trade union activities among *karamcharis*, no great politicisation of teachers and students and no student unions fighting elections with funds from political parties. The morale of both students and teachers was high and the future looked bright.

Things have changed since then. A survey in my old college a few years ago showed that the average number of lectures taken by a teacher had exceptionally low levels, that the college became deserted in the afternoons and there was not as much warmth in the student-teacher relations as before. We have apparently entered the era of

A Personal Narrative

demands and rights as against the era of obligations and duties.

IV

Till 1955 I did not think about research. However a change in the academic values in the university could be easily perceived. Persons with third division careers and who were actually third rate teachers but who had managed to get Ph.D. degrees claimed themselves to be superior and these claims were supported by the powers that be. This was frustrating for dedicated teachers. I was however fully satisfied with my life as a teacher.

But when a research opportunity came, I did not miss it. When Prof. D.S. Kothari who was Scientific Advisor to the Minister of Defence, and for whom I had great regard asked me if I could help in solving some mathematical problems in the field of defence, I gladly agreed to do so. I solved these problems in the same spirit in which I had solved classroom problems and was surprised to find that these results were publishable.

Within two years I had published thirty papers and submitted a thesis of more than nine hundred pages to the university. This naturally had some adverse influence on my teaching work. The extra classes were gone, but were replaced by seminars for my Ph.D. students. My earlier experience of learning through teaching proved useful. For instance I learnt Fluid Dynamics this way, it was by giving lectures to research students. However this time it was not teaching based on textbooks, it was teaching based on research papers in journals. My time which was earlier divided between undergraduate and postgraduate students was now also shared by Ph.D. scholars.

I had no research facilities comparable to what students have today. There were no photocopying facilities and I literally copied about 150 research papers from journals in my own handwriting. I had also to pay typing charges for all my papers from my own pocket.

I had fortunately followed a practice from early days; this proved to be useful at this stage. I had decided right in the beginning that all my income from examinations would be spent on purchase of books. In fact I used to buy new books throughout the year from booksellers and all my examination income cheques were endorsed to the booksellers. At the end of the year, we used to settle our accounts and usually I had to pay something.

Just as my time was now shared by Ph.D. students, my examination income was now shared by typists and the post office for reprints and research papers.

However at this time I also opened another teaching front for myself. Some of us in Mathematics Department of Delhi University had felt concerned at the fact that the knowledge of most teachers was not keeping pace with the needs of the times and some refresher training was necessary. We started a study group which used to meet every Sunday in a different college. This brought the teachers of different colleges together in academic workshops on a regular basis.

In 1958, four of us organised an all-India Summer School for college teachers from all over the country. We invited teachers from all over to come at their own expense to learn and some of us in Delhi agreed to teach. No grant was requested. However when we went to request the Vice-Chancellor, Dr. V.K. R.V. Rao, to inaugurate the Summer School, he was surprised to find that we were spending our money in organising the Summer School. He got us Rs 1,600 as grant from the UGC which we spent in cyclostyling the notes.

Dr. Rao inaugurated the seminar by saying that he considered that day as a spiritual occasion since the teachers had assumed responsibility for improving their own knowledge without looking for help from the university or the government. His message was that Indian education system had a bright future since we still had dedicated teachers. His message is as true today as it was then. No amount of drastic changes in the educational system will achieve results unless the most useful change, viz., of love of knowledge and of students being kindled in every teacher's heart, is achieved.

The Summer School was important, since it was held before the UGC and NSF-organised summer schools in India. Moreover, because of the dedication of every body concerned, we achieved results which could not be achieved by the UGC by spending even Rs 50,000 per Summer School.

We organised six such summer schools. The results were spectacular. Every body who came to these schools went back a more knowledgeable and a more dedicated teacher. I had the same thrill in working as organising secretary of these Summer Schools and in teaching in them as I had in teaching enthusiastic students in my classes.

Later we stopped organising these schools, as the UGC and NCERT were organising a large number of them with generous funds from the NSF and the British Council. Though I agreed to direct some of these schools, the essential spirit of learning was very weak in these schools. In fact in some summer schools, the most important topic discussed was the quality of food supplied by the contractor.

V

In 1959, I got another teaching challenge. The Delhi University started an Institute of Postgraduate Studies (Evening) for employed persons to study for their M.A. degrees. I was offered headship of the Mathematics Department here and I was hesitating. One of my close friends however set me on the right path, "You have always claimed to be interested in teaching. Here is a batch of students which needs the best teachers in the world and you are hesitating." I accepted the challenge and was able to demonstrate that given motivated teachers, these students who rushed to their classes direct from their offices could do better than full-time students. The students who came were no doubt tired but they were highly motivated and motivation is the key factor in the teaching-learning process.

In 1961, I accepted the headship of the Mathematics Department at the newly started Indian Institute of Technology at Kanpur. Here we had the best students in the country, selected after a most rigorous joint entrance examination. It was a great pleasure to teach these bright students. However a new dimension to the teaching process was added here by the freedom and flexibility that we gave ourselves. We adopted the internal evaluation system, and coursewise promotion. The instructor of a course is the complete master of the situation, he can teach the way he likes because it is he who examines the students and gives them the grades.

Here teachers have even the freedom to design special courses and teach these if they can find a few willing students to offer these courses. What I used to do at Delhi University unofficially, I could do here officially. Here I could realise my dream of teaching something new everyday.

Here I have also been able to achieve a better coordination between teaching and research. I always give some courses on the frontiers of research. Even in undergraduate classes, I can inject something of the research spirit and even give diluted versions of research problems since there is no fear of an external examiner. We can here ask even our undergraduate students to read expository articles from research journals or to read parts of advanced level textbooks.

The students are bright, the library is well-equipped and we can assign marks for every work that is given to them.

For most university teachers, there is a continuing conflict between their responsibilities in respect of teaching and research. They are paid for teaching, but their promotions and reputations in the scientific world depend on their research and publications. The salary is guaranteed even if one does bad teaching, but promotion is not guaranteed unless one does publishable research. As such, many teachers tend to neglect teaching and concentrate on research and all the time they have a guilty conscience. The situation is made worse by the fact that students very often do not insist on quality teaching.

In developed countries, students unions insist on good teaching. The unions carry out Students Reaction Surveys and in some universities they go to the extent of publishing their results and grading the teachers according to their teaching abilities. They have pursuaded the universities to give Distinguished Teacher Awards, and to establish Higher Education Units whose responsibility it is to help those teachers who want to improve their teaching performance. Just as professors do research for the sake of peer recognition, they have also to do good teaching for the sake of students' recognition.

There will be a good balance between teaching and research only if there is equal pressure from students and the society on the one hand and by research groups on the other. For good teaching, we should persuade student organisations, parent organisations, teacher organisations, and even political organisations to insist on quality teaching. There should be regular seminars and symposia on good teaching strategies.

While it is true that excellent teachers are born and not made, yet it is also true that every teacher can improve his teaching efficiency significantly if he is willing and if he receives special help in the process. The MIT produced a booklet *You and Your Students* prepared by its best teachers. A Foundation in USA funded a commission for preparing a booklet for beginning college teachers. I have myself been interested in making explicit the principles of good teaching and have written about it.

When I was Vice-Chancellor at Meerut University and students came with their charter of demands, I used to take them to task for not including demands for good teaching, good education and good standards of education in their charter. When they agreed to include these demands, I showed to them that their other demands were such that their acceptance would lower academic standards. I also told them that they could not have good education and good teaching unless the demand for these were the first on their list and that good teaching cannot take place unless students were really motivated to learn.

The whole joy of the teaching process is killed when students in front of you are not interested in learning, when they are interested in getting degrees only, when the only help the students want from you is help in passing examinations by your telling them important questions or by even overlooking their efforts at "copying". The internal evaluation system overcomes some of these problems, but then for its success, one must have full trust between students and teachers and in the present atmosphere, this trust will have to be earned by hard work and dedication. As a Vice-Chancellor, I encouraged formation of subjectwise teachers' associations and encouraged them to discuss the problems of teaching. I also organised a number of seminars on teaching strategies.

During the last fifteen years, I have taught for short or long periods at universities of Arkansas and Carnegie-Mallon in the USA, Manitoba and Waterloo in Canada and New South Wales and Flinders in Australia. Everywhere the problems are the same, a continuing conflict between teaching and research responsibilities under pressure from students on one side and researchers on the other, a feeling that teaching should get more recognition and research in teaching and the teaching processes should be encouraged.

In India we have also had the COSIP and COHSIP programme of the UGC, Summer Schools, conducted by UGC and NCERT, the short term courses under Quality Improvement Programme in technical colleges and the Faculty Improvement Programme of the UGC. Finally we now have the proposal for an International Centre on Science and Technology Education which will hopefully conduct research on improvement of teaching.

Teachers have to love teaching, they have to love their subjects and they have to love their students. In the intangible benefits of this profession, we have the love and respect of thousands of students we teach. Those persons who evaluate the returns only in terms of salaries and place no value on these intangible benefits should not join this profession.

Salvation for the country can be achieved through excellence in education, which can be achieved through excellence in teaching, which can itself be achieved by dedicated persons who consider it a privilege to be teachers. May the tribe of dedicated and committed teachers increase and may the example of such dedicated teachers inspire generations of students to work for the welfare of humanity.

5

Looking Back

M.V. PYLEE

MY entering the teaching profession was an accident. However, I do not regret it. On the contrary, I feel happy and satisfied that I have spent a major part of my life as a teacher.

My first job was at Lucknow where I had done my Master's degree. I spent hardly two years at that university. The University of Lucknow in those days was a truly national centre of higher learning. Students came from all over India. From the southern parts of the country there were at least a few hundred students. In one of the university hostels the southerners had almost a monopoly. The members of the faculty also came from different parts of the country. There were no visible signs of parochialism anywhere, no linguistic, religious or regional chauvinism or fanaticism. The atmosphere was truly cosmopolitan and under the leadership of some of the foremost scholars who taught and led the different departments, the university was indeed a truly great centre of 'light and learning' (the motto of the university), an ideal example of national integration much before we started using that term in free India.

One of the decisions of the university soon after independence was to introduce Hindi as the medium of instruction. Although one of my senior colleagues told me that it was only a sentimental decision and it would not have any practical relevance in the next quarter century, in my own case I found that it soon became a weapon of discrimination. In fact there was a crude attempt through the instigation of a jealous colleague who was a poor teacher to create confusion in my class.

A student got up one day soon after I started the lecture and demanded that I should teach through the medium of Hindi as my English was too difficult for him to understand! Even though I assured him that my language could be made so simple as to make him follow me, he persisted in his demand saying that Hindi was to be the medium of instruction according to the new policy of the university. Fortunately for me, there were enough sensible students in the class; some of them intervened and the mischief was nipped in the bud.

II

I started by saying that I never regretted choosing the teaching profession for a career. I should explain why. I was young when I started teaching. My students were only a few years younger than I was. In fact, a year back, some of them were only my juniors in the classroom. Naturally, I could understand their thinking pattern, their problems, their ideals and aspirations better than my older colleagues. I could move with them freely. They could bring to me not only their academic problems but even personal problems, discuss with me freely and seek my advice and assistance. Some of them even dared to ask and borrowed money from me. All this established a close relationship not so much as between a teacher and a student but as between an elder brother and younger brothers. There was no so-called generational gap that separated us.

In my case that continued for years. Later, when I was teaching in a postgraduate department in Patna University, I was the youngest faculty member. There, again, my relationship with my students was absolutely uninhibited. We freely exchanged ideas and moved in an atmosphere where there was mutual confidence and trust. Perhaps this might have been one of the reasons for the head of the department to choose me to take the final year students for an educational tour, year after year.

The tour took us to distant parts of the country and we spent weeks together in one another's company. I also noted that students came to visit me in my house, spending sometimes long hours discussing social, political, economic and other problems with no inhibitions; this they never did with most of my senior colleagues. Again, there was no generation gap.

During my teaching career in Delhi University spread over nearly eight years, I was the Honorary Adviser of the University Students' Union for five years. The Union consisted of students from all the colleges and the University Departments, over thirty thousand in those days. They belonged to all disciplines. They came from different parts of the country. A good number of them belonged to different political parties and groups. Naturally, it was not an easy task to handle them. In some years we had some serious problems connected with the Union elections, largely the product of party politics. But I could handle them with confidence largely because of the close relationship that I had established with the students as a whole and the student leaders in particular.

There were several cases when Vice-Chancellors sought my assistance to solve tricky problems in which some students and teachers were involved in mutual conflict. I could successfully solve them only because of the confidence and trust the students had in me. Although I was a senior teacher by then, there was no generational gap that separated us from one another and I could boast of being a true friend, guide and philosopher.

It is a difficult task to get along well with students of all types but to be successful, one needs two essential qualities: patience and sincerity. If one's bonafides are recognised and accepted by the students, half the challenge is met. And if one can be patient enough to listen to them and try to understand them, the rest is also met. A little tact, willingness to forget and forgive will also go a long way. Ultimately it is the combined effect of these human qualities that bring success in handling students groups, large or small.

Secondly, a teacher must love his work. Teaching is both a science and an art. One's ability to teach effectively depends on one's mastery over the subject. But depth of knowledge alone will not do. I have come across renowned scholars at a great university like Harvard who were poor teachers. In spite of their scholarship, the students never had a good word for them as teachers. This was largely because of their poor communication ability.

Commenting on this aspect, a Harvard publication once said: "A great scholar may not always be a brilliant speaker. But his presence in the University campus should inspire both his junior colleagues and students." Harvard, however, conducts an annual survey of most popular courses in the university and the teachers who offered them. The survey always emphasises the communication ability of the teacher as one of the reasons for the popularity of the course.

The situation is not much different in our country. The most successful teachers are not only masters of their subjects, they also have the mastery to put across their ideas impressively to any group of students. And such a teacher, if devoted to his work and helpful to his students, academically and otherwise, is bound to become an object of their esteem and even admiration. Age should not stand in the way to maintain this relationship, nor domestic preoccupations.

Speaking from personal experience, I have always maintained a close relationship with my students who are large in numbers. Many of them write to me from time to time, even from distant places, informing me of their change of occupation, position or address. Others send me greetings on the New Year Day or other important occasions. It has not been physically possible for me to respond to all such communications and yet this had been a continuing phenomenon and source of great satisfaction and pride to me.

III

A related question that assumes importance is the possible conflict of a teacher's research interests and the time that he can set apart for his students in addition to his class work. This conflict is more real in the case of college than university teachers. The normal workload in our colleges is rather heavy. At the end of the day most college teachers are naturally eager to get back home. If the teacher has a family to look after, most of his time at home is used up in that process. If he is a conscientious person, he must set apart some time for preparation of his lectures on the following day. If he has to do his work well, even an experienced teacher has to update his knowledge in the subject and remain familiar with current developments by reading journals and other publications. When his domestic obligations are added to this, he has practically very little time for research.

This is the reason why most college teachers are unable to pursue any serious research programme. The few who are exceptions to this statement plan their time and work hard and succeed in research during the early years of their career and earn doctorate degrees and so on. In the case of such persons, there will be no serious conflict between their research work and obligations to their students. They are able to adjust the conflicting claims of both by proper planning and organisation of their work. Once they establish themselves in this manner, they are able to plan their time and produce enough research work which will maintain their reputation in their chosen field of work. However, these are exceptions rather than the rule in the college system.

The position of the teachers in university departments is substantially different. Their workload is much less than that of the average college teacher. Most of them enter the department with a Ph.D. degree to their credit. They work in an atmosphere conducive to research. Many of them have facilities such as library, laboratory and space (for example, a separate room or a cubicle) which facilitate their undertaking research. Above all, most university departments which have a reputation can get funds for research from national institutions like the UGC, the ICSSR, the ICAR, the Planning Commission, the Department of Science and Technology and several others. The very fact that funds are available for research is a great incentive. Departments will also have specialists who have established reputation in research and that helps younger teachers to team up with them. In many university departments, especially in science subjects, students also get involved in research projects. All these, plus the time at the disposal of the university teacher, enable him to pursue research if he is interested and inclined to do so.

A truly research-oriented university teacher can also make use of his summer vacation, at least a part of it, for his research pursuits. Some Indian universities have a summer vacation which lasts as long as three months. If one has definite plans, a good part of this period can be made use of for research and writing.

Looking back, I recall the good use that I made of the summer vacations to do a major part of the work on every one of my books. I used the time for the research involved in those books. During the regular working period, by planning my time carefully, I could make use of the material that I had gathered during the vacation for writing my books, chapter by chapter, first in a draft form and thereafter in the final form. No doubt, hard and systematic work was involved in this process, a lot of midnight oil was burned and many personal comforts and pleasures had to be abandoned. But I feel happy and satisfied today, for it has been through some of my books that I am better known rather than the positions that I held in different universities, including that of a Vice-Chancellor.

The urge for doing research and later converting the product of research into well planned books was one of the early lessons that I learned during my Harvard days as a Fulbright Smith-Mundt scholar in the early fifties. In Harvard, as in most leading universities, the ruling philosophy is, "Publish or Perish". Every year, the annual reports of all the Graduate Schools bring out elaborate lists of all the publications of the faculty members: books, reports, research papers, popular articles, book reviews and any other publications worth mentioning.

A close watch is kept on these by all concerned and the reputation of each faculty member rests largely on his publications in the preceding year. At Harvard, a lecturer or assistant professor is initially appointed for a period of three to five years. During that period he will receive from the university every possible assistance and encouragement to develop himself. At the end of the period if his work has been satisfactory, he is given a new appointment as associate professor. If such a higher appointment is not given, he invariably has to leave the university looking for a job elsewhere.

In other words, no lecturer or assistant professor at Harvard gets an extension in the same position. I have seen how some of the seniormost professors of Harvard, leave alone younger and junior ones, work very late in the night in their rooms at the university. It is a sight one must see to believe. Once a university teacher develops the urge for research and earns a reputation through his publications, he will never stop continuing the work. In fact, it becomes his second nature!

Conditions in many Indian universities are not as conducive to research as American or European universities. But they are much better than those existing in our colleges. And there are many university departments which offer reasonably satisfactory conditions for research for those who are interested. Fortunately our universities give considerable importance to research and the junior members of faculty are rewarded by higher appointments as readers or professors. I have never had to face any conflict of interest between my research work and my relationship with my students. On the contrary, my research work and publications have helped me to maintain closer and more genuine interaction with many of my students.

IV

One would at this stage naturally ask the question why there has been such steep deterioration of standards of higher education in our universities during the last forty years. It is difficult to give a simple answer to this question; it involves too many complex factors. Political independence in 1947 gave a feeling to the country as a whole that we should break off as quickly as possible from the regulations and constraints imposed on us by our foreign rulers. It was indeed a natural feeling and no one could find fault with that approach. But at the same time we forgot the realities of the situation and started acting in a manner which was detrimental to the smooth progress of the country in many spheres of its activities. Higher education was one of them.

There are three categories of persons in the university system who came under the spell of politics which made the entire system suspect. These were the students, the teachers and the non-teaching employees. Today each of them is under the evil influence of party politics.

Let us consider the case of the students first. Prior to independence, especially from 1942 onwards, many students got drawn into the freedom movement. But then, the students were not organised on a party basis. They were only a part of a great national movement which aimed at the political independence of the country. By 1947 however, the situation had undergone a basic change when the Communist Party of India started organising students under the banner of the Students' Federation of India (SFI) and using them for the party's agitational programme. Since the party was opposed to the Congress governments all over the country, the SFI was made use of as a vehicle of propaganda against the government in all the states. The Congress party could not sit by idly watching this development. It was its turn then to organise its own student's wing. In the 50's, with the emergence of more political parties, the number of students' organisations also grew, each one of them with its affiliation to a particular political party.

The emergence of party-based student organisations in the college and university campuses naturally led to the fighting of Student Union elections on party basis. Election to the unions became a major event in the campus and they came to assume all the overtones of elections to the Parliament or State legislatures. Students imitated their elders in the election campaigns that they conducted. Often, there was violence, subsequent unrest, stoppage of classes, defiance of authority and disruption of normal academic activity. Since leading politicians of different parties took positions on one side or the other, college or university campuses became battlegrounds rather than centres of learning.

When I was in charge of the Delhi University Students' Union in the late 1950s, with the support of the Vice-Chancellor and a number of senior professors in the university, we made an earnest effort to make the Students Union play a constructive role. One of the significant measures that we adopted was to substantially modify several provisions of the Union constitution. By eliminating outside interference to a great extent, we fixed an upper age limit for candidates; prohibited students from contesting elections after the completion of a specified number of years of study in the university; exercised vigilance over the spending of funds; audited the accounts of the Union, etc. All these had a salutary effect.

I was largely successful in persuading candidates not to contest Union elections on party tickets. But politicians outside the campus resented it. Some of them actively encouraged candidates to declare their party labels. I remember how a leading party politician once approached me to find out how I could help his party's candidate to win the Presidentship of the Union in that year's election. I knew that he was a very influential functionary of the ruling party and yet I had to tell him that he should treat the Students Union election as a friendly contest between students rather than as a fight between two rival political parties.

At least for some years, I could contain the machinations of such party politicians and keep the Union out of party politics but today all that has disappeared. Almost in every university in India, Union elections are fought on a party basis and campuses are no more peaceful centres of educational pursuit. And so long as the present system continues, emphasis on maintaining high standards will not have any practical effect.

Now let us consider the position of our teachers and see how they have contributed, positively or negatively, to the maintenance of

Looking Back

standards. When the number of colleges and universities was small, the number of teachers required in those institutions was also small. It was then possible to select better quality teachers. Before 1947, it was not a rare sight to come across college teachers with degrees from well known foreign universities.

In the few universities the country as a whole had then, most teachers in the departments were highly qualified in their respective fields. Admission to these departments was available only to deserving candidates. There was good discipline in those institutions. On the whole the teachers were a dedicated lot and the students made good use of the studious, congenial atmosphere in the campus to enrich themselves intellectually and develop their personality as best as they could.

Since independence, however the mushroom growth of colleges and the creation of more and more universities without adequate preparation and sufficient resources, has brought about a qualitative change in the entire field of higher education. As large numbers of new colleges were established, they required a large number of teachers. But they were not readily available. In many colleges, school teachers, if they had a suitable degree, were appointed as lecturers. When some of the colleges started postgraduate degree courses, they could not find well qualified teachers to handle the classes. To meet the situation all kinds of improvisation were made. The colleges had no good libraries, laboratories and equipment.

Postgraduate degrees were doled out to undeserving candidates who were taught by teachers ill-equipped for the task. As the number of sub-standard teachers increased in the colleges and the universities, they began to get unionised and politicised. Political parties also found this situation congenial. Collective bargaining under the guise of bettering service conditions always undermined discipline, sought the lowering of qualifications, demanded promotions not on the basis of merit but seniority in service and less emphasis on research and excellence in quality.

Today teaching is at a discount in our colleges. Teachers and students alike look for suspension of work under whatever pretext they can and often conspire or engineer to create situations which compel the institutions to close down for extended periods. No wonder, under such conditions, higher education in the country has lost its true character and what goes in its name has become a farce.

The growth of a large class of non-teaching employees in our universities in the sixties and the seventies has quickened the pace of deterioration of standards in the field of higher education. Unlike foreign universities, our universities (also the larger colleges) have an army of non-teaching staff. In some universities the non-teaching employees far outnumber the teachers. Not only are they unionised, they also are affiliated to different, rival political parties.

The university administrations have been compelled to spend more and more time and attention in dealing with the myriad demands of these employees than attend to matters which are directly concerned with the academic and related matters in the university. It is not rarely that a group of non-teaching employees without notice paralyse the normal functioning of a university on a flimsy matter in which a non-teaching employee is involved.

The manner in which they make their demands on the university administration will make any outsider feel that the university's primary objective is the interests of the non-teaching employees; neither the students, nor the teachers nor the society that they are obliged to serve.

They have by now formed federations and confederations of their own, embracing the entire country and grown like leviathans, threatening the very existence of universities as centres of learning and enlightenment. Their alliance with unscrupulous politicians who are ever ready to become their leaders and their affiliation with political parties and groups has increased their clout as a potential threat to the university system.

V

Can we redeem our university system from the dirty mire into which it has fallen deep? It is a difficult question to answer. Many commissions and committees have gone into the problems of education in India and how the system may be reorganised and revitalised. But one singular drawback of their recommendationa is that none of them has emphasised the evil effect of politicisation in our campuses, especially in our colleges and universities.

The question whether a university is organised to facilitate the pursuit of learning or that of power has not been answered by any of the committees or commissions although that appears to be the most serious question that deserves a clear and categorical answer in the context of what happens in the university system today. The manner in which politics plays a predominant role in the governance of our colleges and universities makes one feel that we seem to have altogether lost sight of the basic objective for which these institutions have been established.

Politics has become a pervasive phenomenon in the constitution and working of almost all university bodies, academic and administrative, in the selections for appointments, including that of the Vice-Chancellors and other key functionaries, in conducting the examinations, in the allocation of research funds and in the award of scholarships. Politics has been playing a disgraceful role even in the award of degrees and diplomas. Direct political interference is the tendency of the politically oriented trade unions or associations of teachers, students and non-teaching employees, to exploit even ordinary situations in the campus to whip up trouble and disrupt the peaceful academic atmosphere.

Things have come to such a pass that students, teachers and non-teaching employees are sharply divided into different political camps, and issues confronting them are analysed and their approach moulded not on the merits of the issues but on the basis of their political affiliations and often according to the dictates of their masters outside the campus. Every political party in the country is guilty of collusion in this nefarious game which has brought almost every university in the country to a pathetic plight.

There is however a widespread feeling today against politicisation. Most persons, including the students, the parents, the guardians, the teachers and the administrators stress the need to cleanse the universities of this evil and establish the right atmosphere and create a proper environment for useful work. However, no one has a clear view as to how to bring this about. Unless all political parties come to an understanding and establish a consensus on this issue, no tangible result is likely to emerge. And unless party politics is eliminated and politicisation of university bodies is stamped out, it is unlikely that our universities will ever fulfil the role for which they have been established.

6
A Cause and an Opportunity

M.S. GORE

I cannot say that I always wanted to be a teacher and only a teacher. In my adolescent years, like most others, I visualized myself in many different occupational roles at different times. But it would be honest to say that of all the many varied occupational aspirations that I may have had, the one of being a teacher, a researcher and a socially committed person was probably the most dominant one.

I was in my early teens when the struggle for independence was being waged. I was too timid to visualize for myself any heroic role in it. Yet the idealism generated by the movement was such that we all felt the need to serve a cause. I thought teaching provided me with a cause and an opportunity to serve. There was a time when I wanted to go to a village and be a primary school teacher. But I never committed myself openly to such a goal and soon allowed myself to be persuaded out of it and become convinced that I could serve better if I equipped myself with more knowledge.

The idea of becoming a professor, a researcher appealed to me more and certainly fitted my middle class background better. It did not call for great sacrifice, though one could always say that in comparison with entering upon government service—which was then both prestigious and rewarding—college teaching was a humbler career and better met the need to appear to "serve". This need to appear in my own eyes to have "sacrificed" and "served" had always been with me.

I have been conscious of the hypocrisy involved in it. Had I not been so aware I would only have deceived myself. Psychoanalysts may trace it to some basic sense of guilt in my personality, but as a sociologist I can trace it to the compelling need to fit into the social ethos of the 1930's. I am now aware that I have never made any "sacrifices". The most I can claim is that I have not pursued personal gains or sought social status in the garb of appearing to serve a cause.

I have on the whole enjoyed my work and though it is likely that I could have opted for better opportunities, I have no sense of regret nor of righteousness.

II

When I joined college I was a student of physical science. I did not aim to be a doctor nor an engineer. I wanted to be a teacher and researcher or a researcher and teacher; I am not sure of the order in which I perceived my role. But I had dreams of my sitting alone in a laboratory working away in search of—I know not what. It was a daydream. It was a "role" that I saw myself in.

At the end of my first year of science, I found my name in the second class on the result sheet. I was saddened. My professor of English told me that I had topped the list in English among students of both the science and the arts stream. He passingly mentioned the idea that I should probably change to the arts stream and study English. I liked the idea. I now fancied myself to be good in English. In no time my dream of a scientist working away in the laboratory was replaced by that of a college professor and a distinguished writer.

I changed my course and my college in order to study under a distinguished professor of English. I studied hard. My professor had great expectations of me. But, again, when the B.A. results were out I found my name in the second class. This coincided with the year 1942—the year of the Quit India movement. A few of my friends threw themselves into the movement. Most went on to their M.A. classes or found jobs in the expanding governmental bureaucracy. I did neither. I just stayed at home. I did a lot of reading. I remember reading works of Gandhi, Nehru, Russel, Shaw, Maugham and one book by Eddington—a strange medley, but not unrepresentative of my generation.

In 1943, one of my relatives suggested that I might wish to look into the possibilities of a career in labour welfare. If I were interested, he said, I should join the newly established School of Social Work in Bombay. Again, I followed up the idea. I must have been very suggestible. I was admitted to the School, but I soon found that I did not want to be a labour welfare officer. The courses in sociology, psychology and social research interested me more.

Again the idea of being a teacher and researcher asserted itself. This time in the field of social work and social sciences. I did reasonably well at the School and was awarded a one year fellowship to do research on secondary school teachers. But the School at that time did not really offer much training or scope for research. I realized that if I wanted to do research, I needed a much stronger grounding in one of the basic social science disciplines. The discipline that I was attracted to was sociology.

Thus, after three years at the Sir Dorabji Tata Graduate School of Social Work—two to get my diploma and one year on my fellowship —I joined the University School of Economics and Sociology in Bombay as one of the first group of students who chose sociology for their M.A. I finished my M.A. two years later. For once, I had done well in the eyes of the examiners. I had studied regularly, but I had also been so busy with the work of the first All India Conference of Social Work, that I didn't really expect a great deal out of my examinations. My results again took me by surprise but this time in a different, more pleasurable way.

III

My results must have become known in June and by July, I had joined the newly established School of Social Work in Delhi. I had been recruited because I had a professional qualification in Social Work and could also be expected to handle the introductory Sociology course.

I was then 27 years of age. My students were all college graduates and two of them were only one or two years younger to me. While I had looked forward to be a teacher, I had not really thought out what the teacher's role involved and what it demanded from me.

I had a notion that if I knew my subject and could communicate what I wanted to say I would meet my role demands. On the first count I was confident. At any rate I was unaware of my ignorance. I was also a reasonably good communicator of ideas though I could not be considered an "orator" or even a "speaker" of any great merit. I had regularly participated in debates, discussions and elocution competitions in my college days. Once or twice I had even won a prize.

Fortunately, the class size was small and I was not wanting in

A Cause and an Opportunity

confidence. I lectured away merrily. In my enthusiasm—and, maybe, in my unrecognized nervousness—I spoke so loud that I could be heard by passers-by on the road outside the school. One of my friends politely told me that I was teaching even those who hadn't paid the fees and probably did not want to benefit by my lectures.

IV

I enjoyed my teaching in those early years. I don't know whether my students enjoyed it as much. In the late '40's and the early '50's students were not very demanding. They were respectful in their attitudes. Though I was not a great 'mixer', the small size of the student body and the need to interact with students in supervision of their field work brought me into close touch with them. When I look back on those years I realize that I did not use the opportunity really to get to know my students as individuals or to get really close to them.

I think that remained my weakness throughout my teaching career. I saw my students as students, I did not know them as persons. There were, of course, exceptions. There were a few who were intellectually stimulated by my teaching and there were some who responded to me as a person. Some of them have become my friends over the years. The students whom I taught in the first few years in Delhi— before I became Principal—felt free to seek and establish communication with me though I did not often take the initiative to do so.

Once I became Principal, though I continued to teach as many hours per week as before, my authority role seemed to combine with my lack of initiative in establishing social contact and increase the distance between me and my students. Besides, the age difference between me and my students also increased with years. I believe I continued to enjoy their respect and affection; but inevitably I remained a distant figure separated by the authority associated with the role of an institutional head.

A good teacher-administrator should serve as a confidant to his young, erring student who is still in the process of growing up. My inability to establish individual, personal relationships with students also limited my ability to function as a confidant. I had to depend upon some of my other colleagues to play this friendly, supportive role.

If I did not succeed in being a 'friend', 'philosopher' to my students, I was yet generous in my understanding of their problems and I was prepared to listen. Also I never bore grudges or misused my authority to ensure obedience. This helped in maintaining open channels of communication between individual students or student representatives and me. I tried to make them understand the rationale behind the rules that I made as administrator. I did not insist on their blind observance, rather I sought their reasoned acceptance. I avoided the temptation of "making an example" of students who broke the rule and had to be "punished". I was content if the student saw his error and accepted a symbolic or relatively minor punishment.

As a teacher the challenge before me was to make social science—sociology, in this case—relevant to students of social work. One of the dilemmas in social work education is that if you get too involved in a social structural perspective on social problems you are likely to lose sight of the need for immediate action with reference to particular individuals or groups. While an understanding of the social context and the social genesis of problems is essential for social work practice, a preoccupation with social structural analysis can interfere with your functioning as a field level social worker.

Throughout my teaching career I have had to define for myself and for my students the linkages between sociological analysis, social work, social reform and social action. To mediate between an intellectual analysis of problems and the challenge of action in response to social need means mediating between two different time frames—the long term and the immediate. My own training in both disciplines has given me access to professionals in both categories, but sometimes it made me feel an outsider to both.

This dilemma has been paralleled in my life as a teacher by another dilemma—the one of determining priorities between my roles as teacher and administrator. The strain has been minimized by the fact that for the greater part of my working life I have functioned in institutions with small student bodies. It is this same factor that has enabled me in some measure to pursue my interest in research and in writing.

I believe that teachers generally, but postgraduate teachers in particular, must engage in expanding the area of knowledge of their particular disciplines. This may involve field work, laboratory work or just library work. The essential requirement is that the teacher must be intellectually active at the level of concepts and analysis. If he only limits himself to conveying what is contained in textbooks or to purely descriptive statements about the phenomena with which he is concerned he cannot remain intellectually alive and, certainly, cannot stimulate young minds to ask new questions. That is the essence of education and of creativity in education.

V

The teacher has another important role—to reinforce through word and through practice a framework of values relevant to his time and place. This role has to be performed more directly and didactically at the level of school education. But even at the college and postgraduate level the student is young. While he will not seek nor welcome direct advice he is sensitive to the example set by his teachers.

In this area the students' expectations are even greater from administrative heads of institutions. The administrator must be clear in the norms he sets, fair in his judgement, firm in his demand for conformity but not individually vindictive. There is a 'parental' role that every teacher plays to a greater or lesser degree vis-a-vis his students. This aspect of the teacher's role gets accentuated in the case of the administrator.

The parent role that the teacher plays vis-a-vis his students has an active and a passive facet. The active facet is the one where the teacher is expected by the student to befriend him, to advise and help him whenever he has any problems. This facet of the parent role can be played only in case of students with whom the teacher has been able to establish a close personal bond. This happens normally only in a few cases.

But the passive facet of the parent role that a teacher plays is that of serving as a 'model' for his students. Here, minimally, the teacher is expected to behave in accordance with the values that he propounds. Failure to do so will result in the teacher losing his moral authority with the students who have come to look up to him and in a small way to lionise him.

Fortunately, the expectations of the students from their teachers—in this parental role—are not very high. The teacher is not expected to live on the heroic plane. But he must not be seen to be a hypocrite. Hypocrisy in the life of a teacher harms the students in as much as it is likely to give rise to a sense of cynicism in their mind about the "adult" world that the teacher represents.

I formally entered the profession of teaching in 1948. Prior to that I had played the teacher role with some of my class-mates in school—particularly in the final year of school. I was, also, for a short time in 1947, a tutor for students in their research projects at the Tata Institute of Social Sciences. From 1953, I assumed the additional role of administrator at the Delhi School of Social Work. This combination of roles continued throughout my work life until I retired from my post as Director of the Tata Institute of Social Sciences in 1982.

Apart from administration and teaching, I had always sought to keep myself professionally involved and active in the twin disciplines of sociology and social work. Probably, I would not have been able to do this if I had been the principal of a large, undergraduate college. The last three years that I have worked as Vice-Chancellor have been unproductive for me as a professional. I have not written any research paper, nor engaged a single class. I only seem to meet student representatives rather than individual students and teachers' representatives rather than teacher colleagues.

This role of full-time administrator is challenging in some ways and also one which provides opportunity for new initiatives. But the challenge and the opportunity are of a type different from those which I had sought when I chose to be a teacher. In the profession I now get treated like an "elder" both because of my age and administrative position. Co-professionals don't expect me to be up-to-date. Sometimes, when I am tired, I feel tempted to accept this passive, elderly role. Yet, I am aware that that path will lead to intellectual stagnation.

VI

The role of a Vice-Chancellor is a curious one. If he is a person with a background of some academic achievement it may help him to get credibility among the teachers—particularly teachers at the postgraduate level, but his day-to-day work hardly depends upon his academic abilities except to the extent that his previous experience as a teacher may give him greater insight into the anxieties and aspirations of teachers.

As an administrator, the Vice-Chancellor is supposed to be the chief executive. But there is little that he can do as an executive, because unlike a government bureaucrat or a company executive he is an executive-head-in-council. On most important issues, whether they relate to teachers, college managements or students, he can act only on the advice and direction of one or more of the various "authorities"—councils and committees—of the university.

The most curious situation is the one where a Vice-Chancellor presides over a Senate meeting. As a chairman he is expected not to take sides in the discussion, yet as the executive head he is the target of criticism and is accountable for the errors of omission and commission of the administration. It is like a chief minister who is expected to perform the role of a speaker. But a chief minister is elected by his party and the whip can be used to keep the members in toe whenever an issue has to be voted upon. The Vice-Chancellor—except in a few universities—is not elected.

Even if he is, he has no organized party to fall back upon. He is usually an appointee of the Chancellor (and, indirectly, of the Government) but is expected to carry the Senate and the authorities with him in the initiatives that he might take. If he tries to create a group to stand by him in the debates in the various authorities, he will only succeed in heightening the contentiousness of the atmosphere which characterizes discussions in many of these bodies. The contentions, ostensibly, are over academic issues, but often they are around persons or between persons who are trying to establish their claims to leadership and influence.

This is inevitable where members have to contest elections to gain entry to higher authorities of the university. Elections mean constituencies. And constituencies have to be nursed.

Even when a Vice-Chancellor stays out of factions, individuals and groups will occasionally charge him with being soft or partial to some rather than to others—largely to put him on the defensive and make him receptive to their own point of view. If the Vice-Chancellor takes aggressive or even positive postures he runs the risk of giving rise to an opposition group. If he does not exercise any initiative, he will be regarded as weak and individuals seeking to be 'leaders' will seek to manipulate him.

In all this pre-occupation with "managing" various groups and committees, the focus on academic issues is likely to get blurred. It is always a test whether in the midst of all these goings-on, the Vice-Chancellor can keep his perspective clear and also maintain objectivity in his dealings with persons. He has to develop an ability to forget a lot that may not be to his liking and sometimes even hurtful to his ego and remember what it is that he has set out to achieve.

This is not the same as developing 'a thick skin', because a thick skin reduces your sensitivity to important issues and to academic priorities. It is a matter of functioning with a heightened sensitivity which enables you to filter out the inessential from the essential and enables you to keep on working for what you consider important. This is difficult under the best of circumstances.

What has been said above may give the impression that the Vice-Chancellor is the only source of wisdom and sobriety and that he has to fight a lone cause. This need not be the case. In fact, if such were the case, the university would not be able to function. Much of the work entrusted to various committees and authorities gets done because on all these bodies there are some individuals who give liberally of their time and show a commitment to serve the university. A Vice-Chancellor ploughing a lone furrow would hardly achieve anything.

One thing is certain. In the life of a Vice-Chancellor there is never a dull moment. If you have the 'right' temperament you may even enjoy being one. I have great respect for those who have continued as Vice-Chancellors for 10-12 years. In my case the age bar precludes the possibility of a second term. I am content with this situation.

Despite the many problems, there is still opportunity to initiate new, wholesome academic and administrative policies. If the Vice-Chancellor succeeds even in one or two areas he can do a great deal of good for thousands of students and their teachers in the university. But unlike in the role of a teacher where he can see the results of his good efforts within a relatively small span of years, the Vice-Chancellor may not see the fruit of his labours during his term of office.

7
In Search of Relevance

C.T. KURIEN

I was a college teacher for twentyfive years after which I joined a research institute to become a full-time researcher. Being a teacher or a researcher was not something I had originally planned for. In fact in my boyhood plans for the future I had thought of myself at different times as a scientist, social worker, lawyer or journalist. When I was in the high school I was fairly certain that I would do my higher studies in physical sciences in which I was doing very well then. But a definite change came in 1947 when I was in the final year of high school in what was then the State of Travancore.

When the school reopened in June it had become clear that India would become free before the end of the year, but the situation was very different in Travancore. An autocratic Dewan of the state who was very unsympathetic to the freedom movement in the country and to democratic aspirations of the people of the state had mooted the idea of an Independent Travancore outside the Indian Union. Consequently popular agitation was intensified in the state demanding that the Dewan should resign, that Travancore must join the Indian Union and that Travancore, Cochin and the Malabar districts of the Madras Presidency should merge to become United Kerala.

One of the Congress leaders in that locality was a friend of our family and he convinced me that students had a key role to play in what he described as "the final liberation movement in Travancore". The State Congress had called for a general strike in which colleges and schools also participated. I used to take part in elocution competitions and debates in the school and so became the obvious choice as a senior student to address a student gathering.

That occasion was a turning point in my life. For one thing, although I used to suffer from stage fright in school debates, I had no problem in addressing a large gathering of students from many schools, teachers and many others. I was pleasantly surprised about this. Later on a teacher of mine who used to help me in debates and elocutions told me that I was very effective on that occasion because I spoke with conviction and was speaking *to* the audience. When I turned to teaching later on, I discovered that whatever I knew well I could communicate with ease if I concentrated on the listeners rather than on myself. This elementary lesson has been of immense help to me in public speaking also which I continue to do to small and very large audiences in our country and elsewhere.

More important from a long-term point of view was the substance of what I said on that occasion. The country and the state must become free so that the people will be able to find solutions to their pressing economic problems. Of course, it was not an original thought of mine. But I had internalised it, and spoke with conviction when practically all other speakers were concentrating on the arbitrariness and atrocities of the Dewan. For the large public meeting on Independence Day 1947 I was one of the main speakers. I stated that since political liberation had already become a reality, we must turn to the economic liberation of the masses.

The big applause I got made me more confident and reinforced my conviction in what I had said. And I decided that instead of taking up the science course in college I must turn to the study of economics. Minoo Masani's *Our India* which we were then learning as an English non-detailed text appeared to me as a very different book from then on. That was the first book in economics that I read!

I did the Intermediate Course in St. Joseph's College in Bangalore. But during those two years I had very little opportunity to know what economics was all about because there was hardly anybody among my senior acquaintances who was familiar with the subject. When the rupee was devalued in 1949 I was asked, as a member of the College Debating Team to participate in an Intercollegiate debate on whether the devaluation was beneficial to the country. I incurred the wrath of the professor who was in charge of debating by declining to participate in the debate using my ignorance of the subject as the reason. He scolded me and said somewhat pompously "What you do not know, you must learn". I replied that I would certainly learn about devaluation, but maintained that I could not talk about it till I understood enough about it. Hearing about my interest in economics a friend of the family known for her radical views gave me a copy of Palme Dutt's *India Today* which, thus, became the second book in economics that I read.

It was with such "preparation" that I joined the B.A. (Hons.) course in Economics in the Madras Christian College. But the very first lecture in "Principles of Economics" put me off completely because it was on "marginal utility". I just could not see what marginal utility had to do with the kind of economic problems I had come to learn about. I talked to the brilliant young lecturer who was teaching us principles. He appreciated my concerns, but said that he was not sure at all whether the kind of economics I would learn in the classroom would have much to tell me about practical economic problems.

A few days later we came to know that he was leaving the college as he had been selected for the IAS. In a farewell given to him he was rather apologetic about leaving the college and teaching, but expressed the hope that among the younger generation there would be some who would resist the temptations of wealth and office and would stay on in the teaching profession. He added that only such people would be able to evolve economics that would be able to address itself to the practical problems the country was facing.

I kept thinking about what he said. In the meanwhile I became more and more conscious about my schizophrenic condition: I was learning more "Principles of Economics" in the classroom and becoming more aware of concrete economic problems outside the classroom, but the two did not seem to meet. So I decided that I would become a teacher of economics and continue my search for relevant economics.

II

I have given a fairly long account of the background that led me to become a teacher because I believe that one's role as teacher will be shaped to a large extent by the factors that motivate him to be a teacher. Later in my teaching career the question of motivation of the academic community became a very live issue, and I shall turn to it subsequently. In the meanwhile I would touch upon another factor that influences one's role as a teacher, viz., the institution in which one teaches.

My entire teaching career was spent in one institution—the Madras Christian College (MCC) and so I must now turn to that institution and its ethos. Madras Christian College traces its history back to 1837 when two Scottish missionaries started a school in Madras which, after the Madras University was started in 1857, became a college affiliated to it. It had a galaxy of distinguished professors and principals such as William Miller, A.G. Hogg and A.J. Boyd from Scotland and an equally dedicated group of Indian scholars through its long history.

A major transformation of the institution came in 1937 when the college moved out from the heart of the city to a spacious 500 acre campus in Tambaram, some 20 miles to the South. At that time, on the basis of the recommendations of a commission headed by A.D. Lindsay of Oxford, the college also decided to follow a "Hall system" with its three residential Halls becoming the constituents of the college. Each of the Halls provided single room accommodation to about 200 students as well as to some 10 junior faculty members while the more senior faculty members resided in houses around the Hall. Thus the college became a place where scholars—juniors and seniors—lived together with the residential Halls becoming mini colleges having their own arrangements for tutorials, meals and games.

The MCC Campus, thus, became something of a *civitas academia* providing an opportunity not only for scholarly pursuits, but also for experiments in community living. It was also a miniature international community drawing its students and faculty from all parts of India, Ceylon, Burma, Malaya, Fiji, the African continent, Europe, Australia, West Indies and the Americas.

The accent in Christian College was on the allround development of the personality of the students and on liberal education as a means to it. In the Honours courses, particularly, the students were expected to pick up the subject on their own with lecture sessions reduced to the minimum. Students of Economics honours, for instance, had only eight hours of lecture in a week and were expected to work in the library for four to five hours per day and three or four hours in their own rooms. Many of us did it also. This did not mean that one became a bookworm. In my final year, for instance, I was elected Chairman of my residential Hall with responsibilities for organising the common life in the Hall and becoming the representative of the student body.

By the time I reached the final year I was quite sure that I wanted to be a teacher although several of my friends had decided to go into the administrative services. The decision was not very easy because I had borrowed money for my education and there were other financial commitments also and many of my relatives and senior friends of the family had taken it for granted that my first concern would be or should be to solve the family's immediate financial problems rather than to become involved with the country's economic problems.

My parents were more understanding and encouraged me to take up teaching although from a monetary point of view, it was a very unattractive proposition. It was my earnest desire to join the faculty of the Christian College, but when I took leave of the college after the final examinations there did not appear to be any possibility of that wish materialising as there were no vacancies at all in the department.

III

Soon after the college reopened in the next academic year (1953), somewhat unexpectedly a vacancy arose and to my pleasant surprise I received a telegram from the college asking me to join the department immediately. In those days there was an air of informality about appointments. The principal and the head of the department could offer a faculty position to anyone who they considered to be suitable. And the younger people who were invited to join the team considered it to be a rare privilege and used to be proud of the fact that they were joining a college where the financial remuneration was *less* than that in other colleges in the neighbourhood.

Christian college also had another daring—perhaps too daring—tradition: those who had just completed the B.A. (Hons.) course and were taken on the faculty were given responsibility to teach the honours classes, while the older and more experienced teachers took the larger Intermediate and B.A. (Pass) classes. The idea was, as I have already mentioned, that those in the honours classes had the responsibility to teach themselves with the faculty members acting only as senior guides.

I did not have any problems of 'transition'. In a predominantly residential institution I had already 'established' myself and so my 'students'—many of them my Hall mates and friends—knew me well, and because of the informal and cordial staff student relationship that prevailed in the college I did not have to put on any 'airs'. I could be myself and that was what the college authorities and students expected. The only change that I did experience was that I moved to a different residential Hall and had a bigger room with toilet and bath attached to it. I threw myself fully into teaching and the many co-curricular and extra-curricular activities of the college. Those were the days!

For a while I even forgot the tension that I used to experience in the past and which was to become very acute later—the apparent irreconcilability between classroom economics and the economics of everyday life. I was doing well in the classroom and was able to make some contributions to the national debate on the Five Year Plans, especially at the time of the formulation of the Second Five Year Plan. And so it occurred to me that with more advanced knowledge of economics, I would be able to use it effectively for analysing and understanding practical economic problems.

The opportunity for advanced studies in economics came when I secured a fellowship to take up a doctoral programme at Stanford University in the United States in 1958. The four years I spent at Stanford led me to appreciate the rigour and elegance of modern economics, especially quantitative and mathematical economics, but I became equally convinced that some of its basic presuppositions were at variance with Indian reality and that, therefore, a radical reexamination of the teaching and learning of economics in the Indian context was necessary. With this in view, although there were many tempting offers, I was keen to get back to the teaching post in the MCC because I could not think of any other place where I would have the freedom to experiment with the teaching of economics.

While I was away many major changes had taken place in the Madras University and consequently the college. The B.A. (Hons.) course which earlier was equivalent to, and more prestigious than, the M.A. course was abolished. So was the Intermediate course. The Collegiate course was reorganised to consist of a one-year Pre-University course, a three-year B.A. course and a subsequent two-year M.A. course. Christian College became one of the major postgraduate centres of the university with eleven departments, including the Department of Economics, recognised for postgraduate and research purposes. It turned out too that the British professor who was then heading the Economics department had to return unexpectedly because of health reasons. During my brief halt in the United Kingdom on the way back from Stanford I received information—a personal letter from the Principal—that I was appointed Postgraduate Professor and Head of the Department of Economics.

My reaction to the appointment was very ambivalent. I welcomed the opportunity that I would have—which I had not in the least anticipated—to shape the new department and make it a centre of learning and research. On the other hand, a former teacher of mine, a senior person, was still in the department and I felt that the headship of the department should go to him. The real problem, however, was that I was also being concurrently appointed Warden of one of the Halls, which, in the Christian College set up then was rather like that of Vice-Principal as the Principal, Bursar and the Wardens of the three Halls constituted the campus 'Panchayat'. I was very unwilling to accept the administrative and ceremonial responsibilities that went with Wardenship, but as the decision was already made, I accepted it under protest.

IV

For the first time I had problems of 'adjustment', and of various sorts. The Halls continued to be the focal point of life on the campus, but I began to feel that the residents of the Halls who immensely enjoyed their corporate life and activities were forgetting that they were in the Hall *because* they were students of the college. To my horror I discovered that many students—including some who claimed to be 'senior citizens'—were not attending classes regularly, and sometimes stayed away from classes, for weeks together while still living happily in the Halls. I found too that some of them had not paid their mess dues for several months.

I took up these questions with the students themselves and at the administrative level, and started complaining, sometimes in public discussions on campus, that while the Christian College was still very much of a community, it was beginning to lose its character as an *academic* community. "The *civitas academia* has lost its charter", I said in a sharply critical note I prepared about the changing ethos of the institution. Not surprisingly, it led to some misunderstandings about my intentions. But I was to come across situations even more difficult to accept.

Some of the faculty members too were cutting classes, I noted. A good number of them did not show the seriousness of purpose called for in a postgraduate centre, although there were several members of the faculty, old and young, completely dedicated to teaching and research.

I was somewhat disillusioned with my postgraduate classes too. Postgraduate admissions had been taken over by the university, and apart from the 'reservation quota', marks obtained in the final B.A. degree examination became the *sole* criterion for selection to the M.A. course. The university's policies also made it difficult to take into the M.A. course even good students coming from "other" universities. Students who came into the M.A. class scoring good marks at the B.A. level wanted to score good marks at the M.A. level also and expected that the responsibility of the faculty members was to coach them for the final M.A. examination.

I was eager to teach rigorous and relevant economics; the students, by and large, wanted answers for expected questions. In a paper that I wrote in 1964 I described colleges as "unwilling associations of students who did not want to learn and teachers who were not eager to teach."

I must not give the impression that the situation was completely gloomy. There were bright spots and sparks. The faculty of the Economics Department, just half a dozen, gave me full support in my attempts to build up the department. We soon came to have departmental meetings, not to transact business matters but to discuss the content of the courses and other academic issues. We used the resources of the Planning Forum to conduct little surveys and organise seminars and exhibitions which led to many students taking part in these activities. The postgraduate students were persuaded to do small "project works" during the intermediate summer vacation they had for which preparations were held regularly during the first year and of which the reports were presented in the second year. A cash prize given to the best project report (which I paid) became an incentive.

When the first set of students presented their project reports to potential employers as evidence of their independent work, and when employees accorded recognition to it more than to marks obtained in the university examinations, the project work came to be accepted as an important part of the M.A. course in Economics in the Madras Christian College. Above all, because of my persistent demands I was relieved of Wardenship, which enabled me to concentrate on teaching and my personal research which had to be suspended during the years of 'high' office.

I became more relaxed thereafter and was able to do a good deal of creative work and writing. One of the books I wrote at this time was dedicated "To my teachers—many of them my students—who raised questions". I must report on some of the efforts put in during that period.

Faculty discussion on curriculum became a regular feature. After a stage of critical assessment we turned our attention to more positive efforts. The anti-Hindi agitation in Tamil Nadu which led to an indefinite closing down of educational institutions provided an opportunity to do some systematic work on "the economic course we would like to teach if we had the freedom to do it." This was before the Kothari Commission's report came out in 1966 suggesting the idea of "autonomous colleges", but the work that was started in 1965 bore fruit in 1976 when the department completed its work on an alternate undergraduate course in economics in preparation for autonomy that was promised for 1977, but became a reality only a year after that. More about this later.

An annual seminar organised by the Department and the Planning Forum jointly was another new feature. The seminar series were quite innovative in the sense that the papers were prepared by the students under the supervision of the members of the staff and the role of the invited VIPs was to comment on the papers prepared by the students and given to them in advance. One of the annual seminars turned out to be quite an event. The main theme for the year (1970) was the New Agricultural Strategy.

There was first a survey conducted by students and staff in a nearby village to find out how many farmers had adopted the high yielding varieties programme and what had helped them to do so. Papers prepared on the basis of the survey constituted the main part of the seminar. But the memorable event was the final session which brought together the Collector of the District, the Director of Agriculture, the Block Development Officer, the Manager of the Bank which was giving credit to the farmers—and a group of farmers themselves! It was one occasion when the officials were not able to get away with their tall claims!

V

During those years I was teaching Economic Theory at the postgraduate level and the paper on Indian Economic Problems to the undergraduate students. The former was a ritual that had to be gone through, while the latter was something I had deliberately opted for and which I used for my own learning. The department had adopted the policy that a faculty member who started a course for a junior class would graduate with them and move up with them right up to their final year. This gave a continuity in teaching and provided the opportunity for the teacher and the students to get to know one another.

Both students and teachers used to think of Indian Economic Problems as a boring subject. But I was able to turn it into something of a laboratory for practical work. Almost from the beginning of the course one hour a week was turned into a "news analysis" session. Every week three or four students would be asked to go through the newspapers and to report to the class news items relating to economic matters. The class would then make a combined effort on analysing each item. My responsibility was two-fold: first to suggest how the item was to be analysed and what tools of analysis were to be used and secondly to take the analysis a little beyond what the average student was able to do. I remember a couple of occasions when some students were able to point out where my analysis was wrong or inadequate and why. And what a triumphant feeling I had to realise that they had reached such a level!

I recall one instance which came as a shock to me. I used to make it a special point to be accessible to students and used to think that I knew everyone in the class pretty well. Just before a summer vacation I had announced a competition, an essay to be prepared during the vacation on a problem relating to some aspect of the students' home town or village. When the students came back during the next academic year, there were many good essays which I got the authors to read out in the class. The prize went to a rather shy chap who had written an account of the problems of the sago industry in Salem. I congratulated him and told him after the class how impressed I was with his work.

Since that was the final B.A. class I asked him also whether he was planning to come back for postgraduate work. He did not say much by way of reply. Two days later I received a letter from him by post in which he apologised for not responding to my questions and explaining that it was because he did not feel very comfortable in conversing in English. Then he thanked me profusely for talking to him—for the first time since he joined the department, he said. I was first greatly shocked and could not believe it. Then it occurred to me that he was probably right. I was certainly accessible to those who wanted to speak to me; but perhaps I was not making any effort to speak to those who were eager to talk to me, but did not know how to do it. From then on I made it a point to seek out the timid students and to take the initiative to get to know them. I cannot say that I did enough in that direction.

On another occasion, interaction with another student led me to make a major change in my sartorial habits. Hari, a postgraduate student of mine, whose difficult economic background I was aware of, used to assist me as a part-time typist. One day he turned up wearing a very expensive shirt. I complimented him on the fine shirt he was wearing, but remarked also that it must have cost him a fortune. He said that the price of the shirt was about half a month's earnings of his father. I asked him why he went in for such an expensive shirt. He replied: "That is the kind of society we live in. I had to go for an interview earlier today, and if I don't wear a shirt like this, the watchman at the gate will not let me in and those who interview me will not look at me". That, I thought, was a fair assessment of the situation. But he had not finished. He went on to say: "Even you, Sir, who speak so much about poverty and the poor, will just dismiss me in an interview if I am not well dressed". He could not have meant that as an indirect comment about my ostentatious appearances because I had always been simple in my dress habits, and in the college too everyone, including the Principal, was very informally dressed.

But his remarks led me to reflect on my role as a teacher who is always being observed by his students. Consequently, as a symbolic measure I decided to go in for demonstrably simple attire. I changed over almost completely to white khadi shirts and used khadi material for pants also. The symbolic gesture had the desired effect. People kept asking why I had changed suddenly and whether I was coming to have political ambitions! (Those were the days of *garibi hatao* when many "radical" economists were using their radicalism to gain personal advantages.)

In response I was able to use the Hari episode to say how the affluence and conspicuous consumption of the few were becoming burdens for the vast majority in the country. I must add here that at that stage my notion of simplicity had a somewhat puritanical streak about it in so far as I associated simplicity with whiteness, in later years I have discovered that simplicity can be manifested through bright and cheerful colours too, and that to be simple one does not have to put on a long face!

VI

I must now return to the quest for the teaching of "relevant" economics to which I have already made references. Gilbert Slater who was the first Professor of Economics of the Madras University has recorded that when he arrived in Madras in 1915 he was shocked to see that Indian students were learning Marshall's *Principles of Economics* in a "parrot-like fashion". This has continued to be the problem of the teaching and learning of economics in India. Marshall may have been replaced by Samuelson or some other celebrity, or more likely by some Indian imitators of Western celebrities, but the "parrot-like" approach to learning economic theory is still the method even where, or perhaps more so when, the economics that is being learned is more precise and rigorous.

Rigorous (including mathematical) formulations of economics make it possible today to learn the subject much the same way as one learns geometry, as an internally consistent set of propositions and theorems built up from appropriate assumptions or axioms. The bearing of these on real life problems usually ceases to be a matter of concern. I became more acutely aware of this problem when I was teaching advanced economic theory at one level and Indian economic problems at another level. Books on Indian economic problems were essentially ill-digested compilations of official statistics about a wide variety of problems, and almost completely uninformed by theoretical insights. I was trying to remove this dichotomy basically through my personal research and writings. Because of the tentative nature of my efforts I did not think it proper to bring them into the classroom, especially at the undergraduate level. Hence my internal struggle continued.

In the meanwhile the students, and possibly their parents, gave a very different interpretation to the concept of "relevance". To them relevant learning came to mean job-oriented learning. In one of my undergraduate classes it became a live issue once. A specific demand came up from a large section of the class which consisted of about 60 students that teaching at the undergraduate level must be geared to preparing them for jobs later. I passed round to each member of the class a chit of paper in which I asked him/her to indicate the job that he/she wanted to take up after graduation.

When the chits came back we had some interesting findings. The jobs that the students were aiming at included clerical posts, administrative positions, trade union work, journalism, law, business, social service, banking and many more. There were some who wanted to go into politics and school teaching. Surprisingly no one had mentioned that he/she wanted to become an economist! I, therefore, asked whether anyone at all was interested in postgraduate studies, and a few hands went up. But even they were not planning to become professional economists.

The exercise revealed two things. The first was obvious and I pointed it out to the class immediately. If the jobs that the students of a class of 60 were aspiring for were as diverse as was shown through the poll, there was no easy way of making the teaching of economics job-oriented. "Relevant teaching of economics" had to mean something else. The message was quite clear.

The second thing that the episode showed was more indirect, but to me more significant. Few students of economics turn to economics to become economists or even teachers of economics and yet the underlying, though only implicit, assumption in the teaching of economics was that the B.A. course in economics should be a preparation for the M.A. course in economics which, in turn, should be viewed as a pre-

Ph.D. requirement! How subtle is the temptation of the teachers to think that ideally all students should turn out as professional academics, and how disastrous it would be if that expectation were to be realised!

We had a faculty meeting soon after when I reported on this episode and suggested that in thinking of a relevant undergraduate course in economics we must consider what the course was meant to achieve. A rather informal factual enquiry indicated that for 90 per cent or even 95 per cent of the undergraduate students the B.A. degree was a terminal degree. So what must we teach the undergraduates? A cynical view was that it was immaterial what *we* were going to teach them, because *they* were not interested in learning anything. I could not accept it as a factual statement, and I was not prepared for that kind of resignation. In any case, we were there to teach and the students were gong to be with us for three years in the Department of Economics and so it was our duty to make the course as useful to them as possible.

Another implication of our discovery was that at the undergraduate level at any rate it was not necessary to teach economic theory *per se*. But then if we are not teaching economic *theory,* what else do we teach? Some of my younger colleagues, particularly, felt threatened by this thought. My response to the question was that we should try to impart to the undergraduate students certain analytical skills, and from my experiments in the Indian Economic Problems classes I knew it could be done. The real issue was to decide how the analytical skills were to be *systematically* imparted. We discussed these issues at length. After several sessions, preparatory notes and introspection, we were convinced that we had arrived at the focal point of the new undergraduate course in economics that we wanted to design.

It is not necessary here to go into the details of the course that finally emerged. But it may be useful to spell out the rationale behind it. The first was that undergraduate students of economics should not become narrow specialists in economics, that is, the undergraduate training must be thought of as part of *general education* in the fullest sense of that term. For this, apart from economics as 'main', the students should also have a related area as ancillary and an outside area as 'minor'. Developing skills in languages should also have a place in the undergraduate curriculum.

In economics main, the emphasis should be to impart to the students the skills to recognise and analyse economic problems, and because the economic problems they would most naturally and frequently come across were the ones related to the Indian economy, an analytical course on the Indian economy should become the core of the course. In order to develop the skills to analyse, they must come to have a proper appreciation of the institutional mould within which the economy operates on the one hand and techniques of quantitative methods on the other.

The students should also come to have an idea of the evolution of economic concepts and theories with proper historical perspectives. The students should become acquainted with the working of the main economic institutions, specifically markets, banks and the sphere of public finance. A paper on accounting should become an integral part of the course. And finally they should also come to know the logical structure of economic theory or theories.

At first it appeared to be a tall order. But in one sense it was to a large extent reordering of material already being taught, but with a decisive shift in the objectives, focus and approach. There were difficulties too, the most important being the fact that there were no textbooks. To overcome this an organised effort was made to compile reading materials. It was recognised too that members of the staff would have to be reoriented towards a different kind of involvement in the teaching process. Some orientation sessions with resource persons drawn from outside were organised too. It was a major effort and a risky venture. But in retrospect it can be said that it paid off. The course was launched in 1978 and with periodic revisions is still continuing—perhaps the only radically different undergraduate course in economics in the country.

VII

As a teacher, one relates oneself primarily to students. One also has the community of teachers to interact with. In this respect also my experiences were shaped largely by the Christian College ethos. On the whole there was a very cordial and in fact intimate relationship among the faculty members and between the faculty members and the 'administration'—another aspect of the sense of community that prevailed on campus. Hence the Staff Association was very much an academic and social organisation.

There was a University Teachers' Association in the city which was also, for a long time, more of a professional association, than a trade union. But gradually the Association was drawn into confrontations with certain privately managed colleges where teachers were treated merely as paid employees without even the basic rights that workers in industry and trade had. I was in full sympathy with the efforts of the Association to champion the rights of fellow teachers in such situations. But I was always eager to emphasise also that the Association had an equal responsibility to see that teachers everywhere took their academic responsibilities seriously and also strove to deepen the understanding of their subjects and to widen their horizons.

In the late seventies the Association decided that in order to force the State government to implement the UGC scales of pay to college teachers a boycott of the university examinations had to be organised. I was against this because I realised that if the examinations came to be postponed it would mean a great deal of hardship to many students. My personal creed was that where my rights as a teacher came into conflict with my duty towards the students, I would give precedence to the latter. I made my views known to the Association, but without making a public issue of it quietly withdrew from the Association.

Around this time I also found myself totally against the stand that the Association was beginning to take against the granting of academic autonomy to selected colleges. I believed then, and still believe, that in our present context where there is absolutely no possibility of a total revamping of the university system, the only possible way to make any academic progress is to give to college and university departments which are qualified and ready to experiment with new courses and new methods the freedom and encouragement to do so. Of course enough safeguards should be provided to make sure that such opportunities are not misused either by the managements or by the teachers themselves.

One of the measures most inimical to the educational enterprises, especially at the higher levels, is the insistence upon uniformity and it is immaterial whether that uniformity is designed by State Departments of Education or by Associations of Teachers.

VIII

What I have learned from my experience as a teacher is that to be effective in his work a teacher must have an inward and an outward orientation. The inward orientation is related to motivation as well as continuous renewal. It is possibly true about any job that one will not do it well unless one has an urge to do it. My feeling is that it is more true in the case of the teaching profession because although, unfortunately, we have few provisions for formal evaluations of a teacher's work he or she is continuously being observed and evaluated by the students who can easily detect who is serious about the business and who is not.

And students respond warmly to teachers who are serious—not necessarily those who have a serious air about them, and not certainly those who put on airs—but those whose records and efforts show that they are serious about their vocation. One of the things that used to bother me most was to note that many among the teachers were either not interested in their work or were indifferent. It is not necessary to go into all the reasons for this state of affairs, but I would like to comment on two factors which I found to be widely prevalent.

The first was a sense of financial insecurity. I would not speculate on where a teacher must be placed in terms of financial remunerations relative to other professions. My personal view is that it should not be too high because a teacher has many other compensations of an intangible nature. But society must accept the fact that a teacher must not be, financially, a harassed person and that he should be able to provide a reasonable living to himself and his family when he is in service, and should be able to look forward to a life free from financial worries after retirement also. While many improvements have been made in teachers' salaries, I do not believe that sufficient attention has been paid to see that after retirement they can live tolerably well.

A second, and more important, factor that makes it difficult for many teachers to work with enthusiasm is the treatment they get from their "superiors"—the head of the department, the Principal in the case of the teachers in private colleges, the head of the department, the Principal, the District Educational Officer and the Director of Collegiate Education if the teacher is in a government college, the head of the department, the dean and the Vice-Chancellor in the case of university teachers. Many of these posts are held by those who continue to be, or at one time were, teachers. But it is amazing how people change when they come to positions of responsibility which are almost immediately considered as positions of authority.

In any organisation a certain degree of hierarchy is inevitable, but teacher-turned administrators seem to forget quickly that there are ways of ensuring that their colleagues should have a part in the deliberative processes necessary for democratic decision-making. In some extreme instances they also tend to become bureaucratic, autocratic and authoritarian. I have learned from my personal observation that the ethos of the institution in which a teacher works can become either a positive influence or a very destructive factor in developing and sustaining his motivation.

But the inward orientation of the teacher needs to be continuously replenished. I have been a believer in life-long education and when I was a teacher, I used to say that no matter what profession one went into, new knowledge and new skills would have to be picked up, adding that the teaching profession seemed to be the only exception to this rule! The urge to learn and reflect was what sustained me as a teacher. But I know that sloth is the occupational hazard of the teaching profession! Teachers get into the habit of not learning at all after they have become *learned*, which, unfortunately, has a past tense connotation about it.

The outward orientation of the teacher is equally important. By outward orientation I mean the manner in which a teacher relates himself to others, especially to his students. The most important thing to mention here is that the teacher must take his students seriously. There are concrete ways in which this can be and should be demonstrated. The first is to get to know them individually and not to treat them (indeed mentally dismiss them) as a class. Whenever I went into a new class for the first time, I used to introduce myself. Then I would pick up the class register, call out the name of each student and take a good look at each one saying: "I am so grateful that we have a register like this and names have to be called out. How else would I get to know each one of you?" I know that the students were immensely pleased about it.

I know of institutions where for administrative convenience students are reduced to Roll Numbers. But it is a kind of convenience that is not conducive to proper staff-student relationship. Another way to take the students seriously is to pay attention to what they have to say even if at times what they are saying may be incoherent and immature. Of course, those who are trying to show off must be shown their place, with a sense of humour if possible, but anyone who is serious about raising a question or offering a comment must be listened to with all seriousness and a response should be given to the extent possible. In so doing a teacher does not have to pretend to be omniscient. A teacher must be willing to admit what he does not know and accept corrections where necessary.

A major role of the teacher is to be available to students to try out their ideas and views. Where he can enable the students to shape their ideas and articulate them adequately he is rendering them a greater service than when he merely passes on information to them.

A further area where a teacher should demonstrate to the students that he takes them seriously is in evaluating their written materials, especially answer papers written during examinations. For students evaluation is very much a part of their work and learning process, and while they may hate the examination, they are very eager to know what the outcome is. Every answer paper should not only be marked, but be carefully gone through in such a way that the teacher should be able to discuss with each student his or her performance. In so doing the teacher will also be able to convince the students that he is fair in his assessments which is another quality that students expect of teachers.

As a teacher grows older and after he meets several batches of students, he may tend to take students too much for granted forgetting that for each batch of students and for each new student the collegiate course is a new experience. Under these circumstances it may turn out that unconsciously perhaps his professional weariness or even professional maturity becomes a damper on the enthusiasm and curiosity of the novice.

Older teachers must, therefore, be more on the guard to see that they, in their wisdom, do not become stumbling blocks to students who may begin to appear to them much younger than was once the case!

Looking back I am glad that I was able to spend the major part of my professional life as a teacher. I have no regrets also that when I completed twentyfive years as a teacher I decided to move into the wider arena of life beyond the college campus.

8
The Pleasure of Being a Teacher

V. RAJAGOPALAN

IT has been a good fortune for me to have been a student of agricultural economics, later to have been a teacher cum researcher and now to be an institution builder. What a sea change was I required to bring about in my knowledge, skills and attitudes every five or ten years in order to play these roles effectively and efficiently!

In the process, I had to learn to keep abreast of (a) the subject, (b) the purposes and processes of the profession of teaching, (c) the strategies and skills of institution-building and (d) the philosophy and approaches for career guidance and development of my students and colleagues. It appears to me that being a teacher has meant being 'a life-long student' and 'becoming a change agent'. This was necessary for my own improvement, for the knowledge of my subject and my students and for the development and welfare of the country. I prefer to simply say that to be a teacher is to be a student all through one's life, enjoying, sharing and contributing to the thrill of knowing, understanding, discovering and building new knowledge and human relationships.

II

In the 50's when I joined the profession as a teacher, economics was a subject with no special attraction for many students of agriculture. Unlike biology, chemistry and soil science, economics was not considered an exact science. It was thought that a person with a certain amount of articulative skills in language could take any position in respect of economic issues and argue convincingly either way. Generally, the questions in the examination then were subjective and called for little evidence. The belief was that the more the number of pages in the answer sheet, the higher the marks one would get. In addition to these depressing notions of 'economics' the subject was treated as part of agronomy/agriculture, both structurally and curriculumwise. Hence the general belief was that agricultural economic analysis was *ex-post*, merely a post mortem analysis with no useful results to work with. Hence when I joined the staff of the Agricultural College, my first concern was: how to make 'economics' interesting, and 'economic analysis' meaningful and purposeful to the students.

Fortunately for me, hailing from a village in Thanjavur I had exposure to the plights of the farmers and the travails of agriculturists. I made it a point, during my visit to any part of the country, to meet the farmers, discuss their problems, relate my knowledge of the subject to these situations and identify those practical areas in agriculture where 'economics' could be applied for understanding and benefitting the farmers, development agents and policy makers. This, in short, was my main preoccupation. When I look back on those first days, I feel that the first challenge for a teacher is to make his /her subject interesting and challenging to the students and, in order to do so, the teacher should do everything to internalize and develop the subject in terms of practical application.

III

Though I learnt to make the subject interesting, I felt that the students' performance was not what I expected it to be. Further, I discovered that the 'curriculum' given to me for teaching was rigid and at times too theoretical. In a class of 80 to 100 students of varying abilities and backgrounds, I found that my classroom management was not always beneficial to everyone. It was here that I realized the importance of learning the pedagogy of learning-teaching. It was not only that I had to teach a subject but that I had to teach a set of students who were socio-psychologically differing set of individuals.

An opportunity came my way when the USAID Team came to our college in the late 50's for offering a short term course in pedagogy and audio-visual aids. It was then I learnt how to modify and restructure the curriculum and match the methods of learning-teaching to the students and to particular areas of the subject. Pedagogy is as much a descriptive science as any other social science is; but it is true that every successful teaching session which turns out to be interesting, meaningful and inspiring to the students gives the teacher as much satisfaction as a musician or a dancer would derive out of his 'performance'. I feel that every subject specialist should have pre-service and inservice training in the art and science of learning-teaching if he /she were to enter the teaching profession. Amongst other things, teaching too is one of the performing arts.

IV

The commitment and personal involvement I put into teaching and the new found knowledge and skills in the art and science of teaching saw me banking more and more on the method of discussion in both theory and practical classes. While 'concepts' were formulated and reformulated in theory sessions, analytical techniques and skills came to be developed and refined in practical classes. Subjective questions were deliberately raised and debated with the purpose of identifying the pros and cons of the issues raised and to develop skills of analysis, synthesis and application.

In this process, I recognised I was also 'learning', learning how to promote and facilitate the learning of the learners; once that happened, the formal 'divide' existing between the teacher and the taught was not operative any longer. I discovered suddenly that my status as a teacher had gone up and the subject had become prestigious with the students. This was perceived from the students' evaluation of my teaching, its strengths and weaknesses, their suggestions for me to be more effective. A teacher's motivation gets reinforced and refurbished by such candid appreciations that emerge from students. For this, the teacher has to undertake research in pertinent areas, identify problems, select assignments for the students, prepare a schedule of work, encourage student discussion and follow a style of teaching which would facilitate easy and effective learning by the students.

The secret of successful teaching is not teaching of the subject-related information but posing problems for discussions and facilitating the learning of discipline-related skills and techniques. In fact such an approach proved helpful to me even when I went for higher studies and training in United States. I could contribute freely to discussions besides going about my studies systematically and writing my dissertation.

Talking of facilitative teaching I am reminded of the several kinds of 'roles' I had to play inside the classroom and outside. I had to be a counsellor, a lawyer looking for holes in arguments, a friend in need and sometimes a missionary. In the late 60's I was required to play some additional 'roles' also; those of a staff advisor, a warden of the hostel and the like, 'roles' which demanded of me leadership qualities, skills of negotiation and public relations. And this period coincided with the starting of the postgraduate teaching programme and consequently new demands at that level of teaching and, furthermore, research guidance.

Whatever be the load of work that may befall a teacher, he/she should learn to be resilient and keep up the spirit of accepting every assignment in the cause of education. It is only a burning candle that can light other candles. But what a compensation! My students working almost everywhere in the country and also in other countries have given a wonderful response to what I did for them during the postgraduate studies. The remarkable patience my students had with my multifarious activities, sometimes diversionary, and excellent understanding of the subject are a part of my memory as teacher and keep up my spirit.

V

The early 70's saw a sudden transformation in the educational milieu of the Agricultural College and Research Institute where I was working. The Tamil Nadu Agricultural University was ushered into existence and with it the trimester system of teaching and continuous internal evaluation. We had to organize a series of seminars and workshops, develop consensus for operationalizing the system and take responsibility on ourselves to design our curricula, prepare teaching resource materials and breathe a sense of new dynamism and work for innovation and creativity.

All teachers in the university began to buzz with activity—directed towards learning the new system, qualifying for higher level degrees through research, talking up research projects and, in short, behaving like self-motivated and self-directed young learners. We had to generate total dedication and co-operation; and it happened!

Looking back, I feel that there is a sense of achievement in our

Agricultural University system and it is gratifying to note that the other general universities have also started adopting a similar system. But the fact that I want to share with my colleagues is that the teacher should keep the spirit of life-long education, and of acting with a sense of accountability to the system and the development of a learning society through our students.

VI

I have heard people refer to great economists and teachers as 'walking encyclopedias' or 'institutions' by themselves. I realised by the end of the 70's that my students, my colleagues and I had garnered and generated quite a lot of information and cases—through collection, of data, research, discussion and field visits—with which to build a school of thought, nay, an institution to serve the cause of Rural Development. Continuous, consistent and dedicated work never fails to pay; it soon paves the way for institutional development—new organisational structures with new directions and goals for work and service. The Ford Foundation came forward to support our efforts to upgrade our capabilities and services and to establish the Centre for Agricultural and Rural Development Studies for the purpose. Thus, the Department of Agricultural Economics where I entered service blossomed into a centre of excellence for studies and training in all aspects of rural development.

When I entered service I dreamt only of a separate but prestigious identity for the subject of agricultural economics but thanks to my students and colleagues, the dream has become more than mere fulfilment; perhaps I was fortunate and successful in the articulation of ideas and action plans, and in responding to ideas positively and with commitment. Perhaps, every teacher who is 'moved' by a great idea and who would work for the transformation of ideas into ideals for achievement is bound to succeed. Perhaps, in the scheme of things, such a teacher is blessed to be a key change-agent.

VII

It looks to me that 'being a teacher' is to be a change-agent transforming ideas into ideals and ideals into institutions which may spread the light of knowledge and wisdom into eternity. It is the teacher who helps to transform an individual into a person of imagination, wisdom, human love and elightenment, the institutions into lamp-posts for the posterity and the country into a Learning Society. It is fortunate for us to have been born into a country of great teachers like the Mahaveer, the Buddha, Shankara, Ramanuja and Mahatma Gandhi.

Finally, the term 'I' used above is purely expository and it reflects the pride of the profession as a teacher and not the ego of a person. This implies continuous life long learning though it must be recognised that knowledge is limitless and one keep on acquiring it all one's life. What remains significant and satisfying is the pleasure of being a teacher.

9
In Search of Authenticity

C.D. SIDHU

IF I were to live my life again, would I choose to be a teacher? I have no hesitation in stating that I would choose to be a teacher again. I say it after due thought. Before I did so, I reviewed my entire life and peeped into all its nooks and corners, its tumults and disappointments and the kind of human being it has made me. In sum, I have arrived at this conclusion after weighing the advantages and disadvantages of my profession for about three decades.

I hope my repeat choice of this profession will not be the result of sheer habit, or laziness, or lack of information about other careers. True, a domesticated animal comes to love his chains. He may long ago have forgotten the freedom of the wild forest. One can also get used to things. I am aware of this kind of escapism in me—my desire to earn my living the easiest way I can. Yet, going over all the aspects of my life as a teacher, I feel convinced that my choice was the correct one, for the kind of person I am. I will remain a teacher for the rest of my life.

I

Sure enough, there's one side of me that reminds me of all the humiliations I have gone through, particularly during the 1987 teachers' strike. Insults were hurled at my profession from all quarters. The government does not seem to care how our universities are running. Piddling politicians can refuse to talk to the teachers for months. The public can blame us for ruining the careers of their sons and daughters. Our students can hiss hatred at us for demanding higher wages for a work load which is among the lightest of all professions. Lastly, there's the anger, the hostility, of my colleagues against teachers like me who would rather be with their students in the class than with the strikers in their protest rallies.

This humiliation is not a new thing either. It has gone on for about fifteen years now. I have been on the defensive all along. I have been fighting for my right to teach; fighting against the politicians among my colleagues, the criminals among my students, and the callous ones among the administrators.

Teaching is not an easy profession. I have passed through many a tense moment. One such occasion was the strike of August, 1987. After thirty days of empty classrooms, I had to 'apologise' to my colleagues in the staff council. I was going to my class, I said, because I was a "coward"! No, I was not afraid of the wage-cut or any punishment the authorities might have inflicted on me. I was scared of the contempt in the eyes of my students.

All the ideals I stood for, all the dedication to scholarship, to art and culture, to research and writing would ring hollow if, for a few coins a month, I could refuse to sit with my students and talk about our favourite books. Yes, I am a moral coward.

Losing esteem in the eyes of my students, my children—and that too for a few additional comforts or an empty designation—is not the kind of thing I prefer. To belong to the top 3-4 per cent of the nation with respect to income and then to coerce the country to give you more! I loathe this attitude. I cannot kill my conscience. I don't care any more what label you fix on me—a Lecturer, a Reader or a Professor—as long as I continue to enjoy the work I am doing.

To plead this 'cowardice', to break away from my striking colleagues, my neighbours on the campus, I had to muster a lot of courage. The bitterness that ensued, the hot words, the fights, I had to face! I was a black sheep, a selfish brute angling for cheap popularity among students, a sell-out to the corrupt government. Such an experience can be a traumatic experience in any profession!

I have had to fight to earn the salary that I am getting every month. Funny, isn't it? And this has gone on with me for about fifteen years.

In 1972, I wrote a book, *Indian Education: A Primer for Reformers*. It was a detailed case study of the University of Delhi and its constituent colleges. Here's the opening shot:

The sole villain in the tragedy of Indian education is the teacher. Mind you, I said *the teacher*. The teacher *alone*.

Dare I still maintain that teaching is the profession for me?

II

The turning point in Indian education, as I see it, is the year 1970, or more accurately 1967-72. The political parties made a decisive attack on our universities during those years. Trade unions took over our higher education. Politicians outside the colleges decided to exploit the explosive student power—a power that had successfully asserted itself first in France and then the USA. They recruited the teacher politicians to run their cells through their disciples. That marked the demise of the old order and the onset of the present free for all.

I came back to my university in 1970 after three years of further studies in America. Before 1967, a teacher cutting a class was almost unknown. Students wrote homework assignments and took midterm tests as a matter of routine. A certain old world idealism still hung around my colleagues. Students walked as if in a hush through the corridors—awe and respect for their 'gurus' visible on their faces. The staff room presented thrilling scenes of pedants challenging each other on esoteric niceties. The disputants used fat volumes from the library as weapons of offence or defence. Our departmental meetings and evening get-togethers were, amongst other things, stimulating discussions on the art of teaching.

Our senior colleagues would share their experiences with us. Of special value to us was their detailing of the methods used by their teachers. These sessions provided us the training which most of us badly needed. Having overnight become a teacher (the transition from being a student can be quite traumatic), I did not know how to conduct myself and how to cope with crowded classes. Our senior colleagues seemed to be aware of their responsibility toward the apprentices in the profession. Some of them must have been frustrated or angry over lack of mobility in their ranks. A few of them must have found their salary inadequate for the needs of their families. But I don't recall acrimonious debates on these issues in the staff room. I don't recall any trade union activity over promotions and privileges among my seniors for the first seven years of my teaching at Hans Raj College.

Come 1970-71, it was a different scenario all over. Half a dozen teachers of our college had embraced politics as their real profession:

In Search of Authenticity

They held major offices in the political parties in the city. They fought elections and in the process got importance and honours outside the campus. They had no time for reading or writing, little inclination or energy to enter the class. They spent their time in the coffee house, planning campaigns and advising strategies with student leaders. Every party had its gang of active workers in each college and department. This wholesale politicalization of elections to the unions had its natural consequences. The centre of power shifted to the party offices in the capital. The Vice-Chancellor, the head of the department, the Principal, lost their authority. Non-teachers and non-students started taking academic decisions.

I witnessed the agony of the innocent old guard suddenly confronted by the new breed of teachers. They could not understand this new missile let loose on the campus. Granted, these politicians were a minority, say, five out of a hundred. But they were vocal, determined, fanatical. The dumb 95 per cent were taken unawares.

Our principal, the dedicated "Arya Samajist" Shanti Narayan, who used to work seventeen hours a day for the college, was forced to "go on leave" by the ambitious schemers. Our Vice-Chancellor, the renowned economist K.N. Raj, had to resign for reasons not very dissimilar. The seniors stood confused at the phenomenon. They were humiliated out of the classes and the administrative offices. Decision making at all levels fell to the intriguers, the careerists, the time-servers. Teaching, as indeed reading and writing, receded—the last resort of the unambitious, silent majority. Good teaching ceased to matter; either for promotions or popularity.

The present entrants to the profession suffer from neither illusions nor idealism. The conversation in our staff room now ranges around: (a) the privileges enjoyed by the I.A.S. but denied to the university teachers; (b) stocks and shares; (c) buying and selling of houses and flats; (d) arranging loans for housing and cars; (e) which political party is likely to grab the union offices or the next principalship, and so on.

Our Teachers' Union went on the first major strike for 40 days in 1972. (Later it was to score much higher : 109 days!) I was confused and helpless and angry. I was very angry. Fresh from a major foreign university where despite serious student unrest, for three years no teacher had cut a class or missed an appointment with me, I expected my students and colleagues to make use of my knowledge, to exploit my abilities. But that was not to be. Everybody seemed to be conspiring against the genuine teacher.

When thousands go on a strike, engineered by mammoth organizations, individuals are powerless to do anything. All that I could do was to write this angry book on 'how to reform' Indian education. I published it at my own expense and distributed one thousand copies. I hurled abuses at the criminals among my colleagues and students who were keeping the 95 per cent of us out of the classrooms. Abusing everyone around was all that I could do. What more can a person belonging to the profession of talkers do? That was my last big effort to defend my right to teach, to express publicly my desire to do the maximum I can for the salary I got.

III

I am less angry now. I have learnt to withdraw, to break away. I would much rather sit with a single student than address a big union meeting, shrieking to make them see things my way. I feel defeated as a reformer. Yes, I'm talking like a stuffy moralist turned sour! Now my protest takes a more durable form. Instead of merely spouting pious cliches on social evils, I try to write and stage plays about them. I am happy to save time from protest rallies and spend it on doing occasional shows of my play *Kall College Band Rahega* (The College will be closed tomorrow), an uncompromising expose of the rot afflicting our universities.

I am a weak man. There are moments when I am alone in my study and tears force their way into my eyes. I feel I am not needed. I am not needed enough. I love to teach. I love to read good books and talk about them. Writing is difficult, yet I have made a heroic effort to write original books which are in no way money-making ventures. Who cares for my scholarship? Or my twenty books? Or my ambition to write fifty?

I hope I know a bit of my peculiar self now. No false modesty for me. I know for certain that the strongest motivation in me is to write a book that "they will not willingly let it die." This book should arise out of my teaching, be "tested" with the collaboration of my students and colleagues. This I believe to be the true commitment of a person

In Search of Authenticity

who belongs to the calling of Socrates and Plato and Aristotle and the legendary *rishis*. This I believe to be the true continuation of the tradition of a country which has contributed the word "Guru" to the world's vocabulary.

But my bosses and students have less and less use for my talents. And I am not alone in this commitment. Nor is the feeling of rejection unique to me. I know my colleague, Rajinder Pal, is an incorrigible teacher. S.R. Singh is also made in the same mould. They too could teach more and better—if only there were packed classes and students keen enough to learn from them. In a country of dire poverty such dedicated workers remain underemployed!

Were I to name a single factor plaguing our education, it would be the examination system. If I am good enough to teach, I am honest enough to give the final grade to my students. But I am not trusted. I have no such authority over my students. I cannot reward a student for putting in consistent hard work every week of the year. I cannot punish a student for cutting 90 per cent of my classes and not handing in any assignment.

There is no compulsory attendance for M.A. students in my university. About 70 per cent of them sit for the annual examination without attending a single lecture. Some of them manage to secure good marks too. What is the role of the teacher then? He can easily be replaced by *cribs* and help books. If students can get their degrees from unknown paper-setters and examiners, what use or respect can they have for the volumes read and written by Rajinder Pal or Singh or Sidhu?

Our existing system is meant for the Minimumists: for students who can manage degree by studying the minimum; for teachers who can steal their salary by teaching the minimum.

I am bitter at the whole system of promotions and recognition in the profession. Not that personally I have not been encouraged or recognized by my seniors or bosses. Indeed I have got more than my due of praise and affection. But there's the rub. When suggesting 'promotion' to me, my well wishers have only one proposal. "I should uproot myself from my present college and become a Principal or a Reader or a Professor elsewhere."

It is my conviction that these jobs are largely an escape from books, from classroom teaching. Wasting endless hours in meaningless meetings is not to my taste. Selection committee meetings, pretentious seminaring on 'higher education' and the like are not my fare. Lesser minds can do that. Failed teachers can do that. I prefer to devote all my time and energy to reading, teaching and the writing of books. And that too at Hans Raj College, where I have worked for a life time.

For that limited objective, my university has no mode of appraisal or recognition. As a teacher, as a creative writer, I can earn no promotion nor higher wages. The profession makes no distinction between the honest and the dishonest, the real and the fake. Your pay packet will weigh the same whether you teach well or make a pretence of it, write a Ph.D. dissertation or a questions and answers crib. A system that puts politicking or wrangling in committees at a premium is not likely to keep many glued to their desks. It can never entice ambitious young men and women of talent to its ranks.

A house and a car and more money! Would these have made me happier with my vocation? Perhaps. I am not sure. Were these my priorities in life, I would have sought them. Instead, I chose to write the books I wanted to. That's where my major complaint against my profession lies. For writing and staging and publishing fifteen plays in four languages (Punjabi, Hindi, Urdu and English) I have spent more than a lakh of rupees, out of my Provident Fund too. The UGC gave me no grant, my kind of man does not fit into any of its schemes. The university has no favourable word for a teacher who, while teaching books written by Sophocles, Shakespeare, Shaw and Kalidas, decides to write books *like* theirs in his mother tongue.

I surely would have loved to be less lonesome in my endeavour to write books. The profession could have made things easier for me—and for my friends who hold the writing of books dearer than administrative chores. Again, I am happy that I have done it and I am doing it. Difficult or not, I have read and talked about and written the kind of books I wanted to. Only, I wish my father had died a happier man. I can't erase from my mind the indictment of my profession the dying man inflicted on me—the man who had made an "honest" teacher of me to start with.

Like all only sons, I was in perpetual conflict with my father. For me he is not dead. He's ever up and about—commenting on my career, evaluating my doings, and (the stingy shopkeeper that he was) calculating the loss and gain. To him, I was a failure—failure as a father to my children, failure as a member of the large joint family of landless labourers. Of course, he was proud of all the scholarships I had won. He had gone to the shopkeeper in his *bazaar*, newspaper in hand, boasting of the prize my *Bhajno* had won.

But materially, what had I to show to his community? Had I been in the I.F.S./I.A.S. (I had competed and secured a top position but a minor medical anomaly came in the way), had I been a lawyer or an engineer or a business executive, I would have provided more comforts to my wife and children and some help to my poor relations. But at 40 plus, after three years of grind in a foreign land, after two decades of teaching at a premier university, what had I to show to my father as my achievement? A few books and their glowing reviews?

Three days before my father died, June 1, 1980, I was sweating, shirtless, in the verandah devising exercises for my students. My father joked with me, "*Kaka*, if you cannot afford a shirt, I can buy one for you". Whenever I remember my father's dying words to me, I cannot help feeling a martyr to the trade of the readers and writers of books.

A father who had started life as a labourer, whose dream was to scrape every *paisa* and send his only son to college, a father who used to seek commitment from his son "not to betray" his landless relatives, had that father not bought clothes and books for his son and grandchildren for eighteen years, his son would not have been able to teach honestly and write authentically. The frozen truth remains that, in spite of my Spartan habits, on my salary as a teacher, I have not done much for my family or for my afterlife as an author.

Still, I would love to be a teacher all over again. Whining against imaginary poverty or neglect, complaining against my students like a broken hearted Lear, will not take away from me the glorious time I've had and the enormous affection showered on me by my students.

Were I to live by bread alone, selling of stamps at the post office would have done as well. Or the selling of shoes, as my father did. Man to man, I grant that *Lalaji* felt happy when exercising his persuasive skills or the poetic art of little falsehoods. When he succeeded in ensnaring his victim in a deal, he was, at the very instant, richer by a couple of rupees too. But the range of a salesman's faculties is narrow. Few activities can rival teaching in providing opportunities for expression of one's total self. Few careers can satisfy the soul as much as the teacher's skill of 'forming' the minds of boys and girls.

A good class is a creative experience. A good lecture for me is one that I have mentally delivered many a time before it is actually delivered. I rehearse it during leisure hours, while travelling in buses, while going on long walking tours through villages during vacation time. At its best, a teacher's performance is a one-man show by a veteran actor. A lecture, like a well-made play, has its beginning, its climax and its end. It thrills me to keep the attention of my 'audience' tied to what I say and do in class. The various creators in me, all the arts at my command, must come into play to make it an occasion for delightful instruction.

The first thing a student may find on entering my class is a list of my major points on the blackboard. There may be a teasing question or a puzzling figure or a clumsy cartoon. I like to grip the students by their necks. And grip myself too. I hate to wander too far from the key words on the blackboard. The class must know where I'm going, what I am leading to. These points are the only notes I carry to the class. If I can't remember things by heart— including some lengthy quotes from the text—if the words or facts from the book have not impressed me enough to get them on my tongue, I cannot expect my students to learn them by heart. What cannot enthuse the teacher is not likely to turn on the class.

Of course, not every lecture can be a *tour de force*. Nor can every lecture be an unforgettable experience. Yet, at its best, the teacher's art can combine the finest elements of arts of the public speaker, the debator, the story-teller, the actor and the drama director. Teaching must be a pleasure. Most teachers of the old school were unsmiling Rodin thinkers, too solemn, too pompous. I hate to be bitten by this awful solemnity bug—that the whole thing is so sacred!

I am not all-wise, nor a know-all. I like to be my ordinary work-a-day self with my students. No pretentions for me, no false front. I hate certain things and types of people. I love some things and certain people. They can take me as a model in the things they like in me, and they can take me as a warning in the things they dislike in me. My own true self, that's what I always must be with my students. I don't want them to put me on any romantic or idealistic pedestal. I'm with them because I enjoy being with them.

But I am not in the entertainment business. My lecture must not be a series of humorous anecdotes, a string of jokes signifying nothing. I am the son of a miserly shopkeeper after all. I want my students to carry something home from each sitting with me. That's how I discovered the trick of neatly putting the high points of my lecture beforehand on the blackboard. I may even distribute the synopses of lectures weeks ahead.

I owe this excellent practice to my teacher late P.E. Dustoor, and my teachers at Madison, Wisconsin. I was a student of Professor Dustoor for two years. Additionally, he gave me many a good tip on teaching over a patient session of three hours. Though an exceptionally witty person, I was surprised to find that he disapproved of witty teachers—who prided themselves on being entertaining speakers on all occasions and on all subjects. Teaching is hard work and meticulous research work, he said. A sense of humour in the teacher can relieve many a dull and tense moment but in every lecture some new fact or insight must reach the student's notebook, if not his head. Thanks to Dr. Dustoor, I chose the quiet, unassuming industrious Mr. Matthew as my role model, rather than his famous witty brother-in-law, Mr. V.V. John.

Not a mere entertainer, I may even be a sadist. I love to play the vexing Socrates, as my Political Science teacher, R.S. Mehta, used to do. Framing harassing questions on the topic under discussion is the sole secret of involving the intelligent students in class work. Playing the devil's advocate helps as much. If you pretend to defend the wrong side, your students will take immense delight in proving you wrong. Once you have succeeded in making the students quarrel over what you are saying, you can be sure that they will explore it in depth on their own, today or tomorrow.

I have been lucky in the choice of my subject too. The teaching of literature and language lends itself to varied methods and techniques. I do not have to reel out mind-boggling statistics or technical terms with outlandish spellings. A hand-out or two will take care of all the names and dates or bibliography; and leave me free to strum the strings for the dominant theme of the day.

Literature provides special fun in an undergraduate class. With them I am more of a drama director. I like my students to get into the situation that the characters of our play or novel are caught in: to become the hero or the villain, let's say. The other students can interview him for their newspaper or the radio or TV. The protagonist and the antagonist can fight it out in their own words in a real life drama. Or, a character can explain his motives and narrate the story from his point of view. Indeed the variety of exercises is as inexhaustible as the teacher's imagination.

Not to let staleness get in, I like to teach new authors and books as often as I can wrench them out of my colleagues' hands. I hate to be the butt of the old joke about college teachers being 'great dictators', dictating, over forty years, the notes that their teachers had dictated to them at the end of the nineteenth century.

V

My experiments with teaching are the brightest spots in my life. My classes have provided me countless happy hours and days and weeks. There was this class of 1966. I attended a six-week UGC sponsored summer institute where we learnt some new methods of teaching English to weak college entrants. Encouraged by Professor Sarup Singh, the head of the department, we tested the methods with 250 students in an intensive course. For thirty days, my colleagues P.S. Verma and K.G. Verma and I taught with a passion, with a frenzy, that few can attain. For one month's honest work, we have been getting thanks from our students for over twenty years. But the students were not the only beneficiaries of the course. My head appreciated the work I had put in and packed me off on a Fulbright fellowship. Who says there are no rewards for teaching?

I am not done with that hard working class of 1966. I wrote drills and dialogues to make them shed their habitual errors. These lessons later became a part of my workbook, *An Intensive Course in English* (Orient Longman). Commissioned at first by my university, it has served as a text in many parts of the country.

Apart from fetching me money for my creative writing and theatre work, this book often helped me to answer back my father. In 1962, sitting amidst my elders in the village in Punjab, I was boasting of the glories of lecturing at Delhi University. I said, "I'd much rather not sit for the I.A.S. exam, as you wish me to. Lecturership gives me a good salary plus enormous leisure to read or write or make extra money." And the conclusive point! "A boy or girl may fail or pass, no blame can come to the teacher. A college lecturer has no responsibility whatsoever to anybody."

The fat was in the fire. With anger and contempt shooting out of his eyes, my father said, "If you don't care whether your boys and girls pass or fail, what the blazes are you drawing your salary for? Have you ever talked to their parents? What would they say if they were to find out that the teachers don't give a damn for the lives of their children? Look at that tailor, Karam Chand. All his life he has lived in chilling poverty. His life's one mission is to see his son through college. Karam Chand will go hungry and barefoot but he must pay for his son's college fee. All his dreams of getting bread for himself and his wife (I am translating from my mother tongue, Punjabi) in their old age are embodied in that child. And you and your colleagues think you don't care whether Karam Chand's son succeeds or fails!"

Bless my father for insulting me! Nothing is as educative as an occasional knock-out by a parent or a teacher. Never again have I been able to look at a boy or a girl as a mere Roll Number. To me he is a walking dream of his parents. In himself, he is a universe of dreams, of fears and ambitions and hopes. Far be it from me to shatter this dream, to stunt this child through neglect or humiliation or discouragement. Not without reason did the ancient Indian student pray for a 'guru' who had children of his own. And living children too!

But what do I do about the children of the rich who are in college only to have a good time? They destroy the discipline of my class and take the lead in strikes and agitations. They cost the deserving ones their careers. I feel helpless. I cannot keep them out of the college. Over the years though, I have learnt to keep them out of my teaching plans. I work for those who need me. "Fit audience find, though few." While writing my books, I keep in mind the millions of poor parents and their sons and daughters. It was for them that I worked hard for months to compile exercises on English grammar.

Had I written an article on *Hamlet* for a scholarly journal, I might have earned a footnote or two in unread quarterlies. But that would not have satisfied me, nor my father's soul. Scholarship and research divorced from the elemental needs of the millions in my motherland are not for me. The humble few in my class need me. I will do my bit for them. Above all, I must be satisfied that I am doing my honest best for them.

Does India need English? Should I waste my life by perpetuating this colonial heritage? Wouldn't any other subject have made my teaching more worthwhile? Such questions do not vex me. To associate a teacher with a particular subject is to misunderstand his role in the life of a young person. I often go over my own life and wonder about what is left with me from my school days. Do I feel grateful to Masters Gobind Ram, Atma Singh and Baldev Singh because they 'informed' me of many things? A lifeless book could have given me that information. Did they try to 'reform' me according to certain ideals of conduct? An illiterate priest could have done that more ardently.

By contrast, why do I hate the very memory of Masters Surjeet Singh and Rajinder Singh? Is it because they wanted me to 'conform' to the tenets of their fanatical sect? Is it because they repeatedly humiliated me for my birth in a community of landless labourers? Were they my sincere wellwishers when they tried to teach me to hide my humble origins by growing long hair?

Indeed the subject a teacher specializes in is the first thing to slip out of a student's mind over the years. Ultimately, what I teach my students is the kind of person I am. I project my SELF, my peculiar personality.

Without Master Gobind Ram's instruction, I could not have chosen Shakespeare and Kalidas and Homer as my life long companions. But that is not saying much about a man who gave me a study room in his house for ten years, who gave me books and food, love and companionship, as few fathers can. He accepted what I was, admired what I did. He "formed" the man I was struggling to be. After all the 'facts' are forgotten, the information has grown out of date, what I remember of Master Gobind Ram's instruction to me is: a human being can do this much for someone else's child!

"How I live. And how you can live." Essentially, this is the subject that all teachers teach.

VI

My self-conceit often gets on my nerves. What *I* do for my students! I! I!! How about the students' contribution to my life?

A fair judge may find that a teacher owes as much to his pupils, if not more. I certainly do. It's they who gave me my life's work: the use

In Search of Authenticity

of the stage for my teaching and writing work. The dialogues I wrote for drilling grammatical points made my classes so exciting, I decided to extend my role into that of a dramatist. I employed the engrossing dramatic techniques to the teaching of novels and poems as well. The next logical step was to 'stage' the prescribed texts for invited audiences. My boys and girls staged Sophocles' *Antigone*, Plautus's *The Pot of Gold*, Shakespeare's *Macbeth* and *Much Ado*, and Arthur Miller's *All My Sons*.

Now, my wife could run the family business of teaching through the stage as an equal partner. So could her daughters. Some colleagues and their families too joined us. [Let's quietly forget the hostile wretches, the envious insects, the bitchy fundamentalists who complained against me to the Governing Body that I was 'spoiling the character' of the girls and desecrating the college temple (where I did the rehearsals) with my anti-Hindu plays.] The rehearsals, the learning of lines, the posters, the properties, the costumes, the make-up, the sets, the shows, the clapping, the photographs, the mistakes, the quarrels, the jokes, the parent-teacher exchanges—it was one big carnival for weeks. And every boy and girl would know the *entire* textbook by heart!

To do things together as a team, to do pleasurable and instructive things together as one big family—I can conceive of no wiser or better way of living this kind of life. And this truth I discovered while experimenting with my classes. About ninety shows of *All My Sons* in six years at twenty colleges in all parts of the capital! On makeshift stages, too: on the lawns, in the classrooms, in the corridors.

My student-actors felt great. They were helping their fellow students in their studies. What appreciative audiences we had, what admiring glances—from boys and girls from less privileged schools and neighbourhoods. Their classmates from Hans Raj College could speak out the complete text from memory for two and a half hours. To many, crushed by a foreign tongue, it was a miracle. Amidst all the strikes, politicking, cynicism and chaos, I could collect hundreds of students together for a compelling performance. Often, when the show was on, I would stand at the back of the stage with eyes full of tears, tears of gratitude to my disciplined and dedicated team. Rarely have my wife and I known moments happier than those when the show is on.

Now I consider myself exceptionally successful as a teacher; my students take over the class entirely. The second year Honours class did, last year. Sixteenth century English poetry is not a big draw for students, or, for that matter, the teachers. I noticed some talented budding poets. I challenged them to play the teacher to their classmates, explicate a lyric or a sonnet. About fifteen braved it.

To my dismay, I discovered that Maunica and Sanjay and Sangeeta taught better than I could have ever done. They wounded my writer's vanity too. In a generous moment, I announced cash prizes for the translation of the English sonnets into sonnets in their mother tongue. I was flooded with entries; and lost more than a hundred rupees. The college magazine editor was happy though; he had got excellent stuff without having done anything to procure it.

I regret to say I have my lapses. Like my crime against Rajpal Ravi in 1983.

I was teaching the first two books of Milton's *Paradise Lost*. The students were reading as different characters, as Satan, Beelzebub, Moloch and Milton. They were obviously involved in the epic conflict. At the end of one such reading, Rajpal stopped me in the corridor. He too wanted to read. I noticed he had the text in braille. What a blind man I had been! As if he were only a listening machine.

I asked Rajpal to read Satan's role in the next class. He must have practised in his hostel room for hours. It was a star performance. There were spontaneous bursts of thunderous clapping every time he finished a speech. I broke down—and begged pardon of Rajpal for not 'seeing' him for a year and a half.

Next morning, I ventured another idea. I carried three copies of the complete epic to the class. I said, we could reverse Milton's process and turn his lengthy dull epic into a short interesting play. I suggested a tentative scene division. Immediately, two students offered to read parts of the long epic and write the script. The roles were assigned, the cramming started.

Rameshwar created a crisis. He said, Milton's lines for Michael were ineffective. He could turn out better blank verse himself. The script writers were furious and uncompromising. They wanted no cheeky poetaster to out-Milton Milton. I delivered the judgement: The world has Miltonized enough for three centuries. It's Rameshwar's turn now. Michael shall speak the verses written by Rameshwar.

Two weeks of ecstatic activity, of frenzied absorption. The class gave a seventy-minute performance of *Paradise Lost*. Rajpal Ravi played our hero, the Satan. He spoke 40 per cent lines of the script, and took his exits and his entrances unassisted. At the annual prize-distribution function, when Rajpal walked up to receive his prize for acting, there was clapping in the hall which will reverberate in my ears to the end of my days.

Over a decade now, my students have been running our Collegiate Drama Society. I overhear Rampu and Ilaksha boasting to this year's initiates how they did the show eight years ago. The group helps me write my plays. They criticize them, improve them, stage them. They have eliminated me as a director. Threats have appeared that soon I am going to be outdone as a script writer too. I am not sure any more who teaches whom.

I grow old year by year but the crowd in my college is always the same age. Not a little of their youthful zest, their fun and frolic, their love and laughter, rub off on me. I wish to be with them, as their teacher-turned-student, to the end of my days. And, if myths are real, when I meet Masters Gobind Ram, Atma Singh, Baldev Singh, Mr. Matthew—and Lalaji—somewhere in the shadows, I wish to be truthfully able to tell each one of them: I could not do for my students half as much as you did for me. But, Sir, I tried. I tried hard.

10
Grappling with Problems

KRANTI JUJREKAR

EVERY human being likes to dream before he comes face to face with a real situation. I was no exception to it. My dream was to pursue research after completing my postgraduate work. But when I completed it and approached one of my teachers to act as a guide, he advised me to change my mind. It would be more correct to say that he persuaded me to change my mind.

According to him, spending some years in research would mean postponing the adoption of a professional career for someone like me who did not wish to continue her research beyond a few years. Meanwhile, I got an offer for the job of a demonstrator in one of the colleges. Though I had some misgivings, I accepted it as a stepping stone till I got something better. But I had another fear in my mind and that is what discouraged me from taking the decision to join the teaching profession.

That fear was about the uncertainty of tenure. When I joined the college I heard that one particular teacher had been kept temporary for nearly ten years and had then been removed. Keeping people temporary for several years was a widespread practice in the college I joined and indeed in several other colleges. Nevertheless, disregarding the uncertainty involved, I joined the post offered to me.

Even though I was not interested in continuing with the profession in the beginning, I changed my mind after a while. The company of young students, their eager faces and their enthusiasm to learn about new things and so on attracted me to teaching. The uncertainty of the job was there all the time. In a sense it was a kind of sword hanging on my head but then I trusted to my competence and to my luck.

From the very beginning, it has been a part of my nature to fight against injustice. Even in that uncertain position, I started organising teachers against the evil practice of keeping them temporary for long stretches of time. In those days, teachers used to be reluctant to come forward and fight against this form of injustice. I remember once we organised a protest day on this issue, the main demand being statutory security of service. As a mode of protest, we decided to wear black badges for the whole day even while teaching in the class. Some of us were sitting in the common room when, on that particular day, the Principal happened to enter along with some guests. One lady from among the guests enquired what was the protest about and what were our demands. In response I explained our point of view.

Afterwards the Principal called me to his office and asked me why I had exhibited the badge in the manner I had done. I was surprised by such a question and simply replied, "It is for exhibition, Sir". When I returned to the common room, I found that all teachers had removed the protest badges. The entire episode filled me with disquiet. What kind of an image would we the teachers have in the eyes of the students if we displayed such a cowardly attitude! It was after years of efforts, mine as well as that of so many other colleagues that this picture began to change. The earlier atmosphere totally disappeared and now teachers speak frankly and fearlessly.

II

I still remember my first day in college when I had to supervise a practical class. I entered the laboratory but did not choose to go around. For quite some time I just remained seated in the chair and dared not move even in order to explain the experiment that the students had to perform. But after sometime I was forced to do so.

One of the students wanted me to help because he had some difficulty in being able to undertake the qualitative test of one of the radicals. This was a Chemistry practical and that was my field of specialization. I went to his experiment table, performed the test myself and showed him how it was to be done. The student felt happy and I also felt satisfied; I too had passed the qualitative test conducted by the student on me.

In science practicals, a teacher faces the challenge of having to get the right results. Lecturing about theory is one thing; to prove what is said through laboratory experiments is another and herein lies the real test of a science teacher. I developed the practice of performing the experiment myself before I arranged them for the students; this was a part of preparing for performance in the class. I had to develop the technique of performing the experiment as well as the precautions that had to be taken in order to perform it successfully.

I quite realised that these efforts of a single person were not going to improve the quality of practical work. At the same time it was important to note that in connection with experimental work, both at the undergraduate and the postgraduate levels, special attention needs to be paid to improve the quality of practical work. Not only that, it is equally important to integrate it with the learning and acquisition of theory. Perhaps it would be a good thing if every teacher before embarking upon his work in the classroom were to be given a short course in basic laboratory technique and workshop practice.

Students in all science subjects should have some knowledge of the theory of errors, the basic statistical concepts and the statistical design of experiments. While entering my teaching career, I still had at the back of my mind the memory of my college days. I can recall two or three favourite teachers of mine, one of whom had created a lasting impression on my mind. This teacher used to stand behind the student while the experiment was being performed. To get an accurate result is important for the student not only in order to secure good marks in the examination but also to develop the technique and the skill of doing experiments. No less important is the correct way of handling the apparatus.

Sometimes students even after they have graduated do not know the correct method of handling burettes, pipettes etc. While draining pipetted solutions, students still blow the pipettes which is what they should have learnt to avoid. When students pass out and go either for higher studies or research or join the industry, it helps them enormously if they had cultivated the correct habits of work.

Why does it happen this way? Why are students not properly instructed? Who is responsible for this situation—the teacher or some other factors? I have long asked myself these questions and my answer is that nowadays, right from the nursery to the college level, teachers have to handle a very large number of students at a time. In technical language this is known as the student-teacher ratio. For quite some time now, this ratio has been against good teaching. How can one teacher instruct and guide 20-25 students in the laboratory? Individual

Grappling with Problems

attention is necessary; otherwise errors cannot be avoided.

As I mentioned earlier, it is important to have some theoretical idea of errors and the possibility of errors. I find that most teachers do not understand what is at stake and therefore cannot even explain what requires to be guarded against. Students for the most part blindly follow what the teachers tell them. The whole exercise is examination-oriented and there is little attempt to understand and to learn.

The experience in mofussil college is even more shocking. I happened to be an examiner for practicals in one such college. I was requested to set only such experiments which their students had performed. On inquiry I found that they had hardly covered half the syllabus. On further inquiry I found that the main reason behind it was the non-availability of those instruments which were somewhat costly. Even the ones which were available were not in working order. Repair facilities were not within reach and therefore the instruments were not in working condition.

Not satisfied with whatever I had found out, I tried to probe further. In informal conversations, some of my colleagues from these moffusil colleges narrated even more amusing stories about practicals being conducted in odd circumstances and so on. The more I heard about it, the more shocked I felt. Why were conditions so bad in these colleges? Are they bad in all such colleges? It appears to me that these are particularly bad in those colleges which were started in the last decade or so and are run by private managements on a non-grant basis.

Clearly the starting of such colleges had been politically motivated. While poor resources are a cause of low standards in any case, science teaching is affected in particular. These colleges could not provide well-equipped laboratories. Even preliminary requirements like tap water and bunsen burners were not provided. In some of the colleges, in place of these burners wick stoves or even spirit lamps were provided and instead of regular water supply, buckets of water were kept. In this situation how could experiments be performed properly. What is required is sootless flame and continuous flow of water. It is difficult to imagine how students trained in these circumstances can acquire the right kind of skills.

III

Lecturing to the class is altogether different from demonstration in the laboratory. Before joining the profession no special training is given to college teachers. At the school level, training qualifications are insisted upon but not at the college level. In consequence, the college teacher does not understand the psychology of his students, how they should tackle or approach a topic if there are any special techniques which can be adopted to keep the attention of students? Teaching is an art without question. Some people may be born with it but others have to acquire and cultivate it.

When I was to lecture for the first time I prepared my subject well, indeed as well as I could. But when I actually started lecturing I found that I was omitting several points and in any case the lecture was delivered so fast that while I had prepared for a lecture lasting 45 minutes, I got exhausted within 30 minutes. What to do with the remaining fifteen minutes? I did not know and started perspiring. Not knowing what else to do, I left the class before the time was up. Feeling upset at what had happened I discussed the problem with an older colleague. He advised me somewhat but the best advice which he gave me was to recall the method adopted by my teachers. This was a useful tip. It helped me to improve my teaching. For I started doing the same things now which had impressed me in my teachers when I was a student.

If a student gets impressed by a particular teacher, he picks up his style, even his pronunciation sometime. I cannot forget an incident. One of my postgraduate teachers again and again asked me to pronounce the word "Toluence". I did so and then he asked me whether I had been a student of a particular professor. I was surprised to find that he could identify the name of my teacher. Everything became clear to me when I learnt from him that he too had been a student of the same teacher. I had picked up his peculiar style and that is how this teacher of mine was able to trace the link back. For my part I was very fond of that teacher and his style was a model for me.

Altogether I would say that I followed the method of trial and error. Even today I continue to do the same. For instance, I found that even postgraduate students expected a teacher to give notes, and those also elaborate ones, so that students do not have to refer to textbooks. In the beginning of my career I was reluctant to give notes. One of my teachers who had made a strong impression on my mind never used to give notes but we still attended his lectures very regularly. His lectures were very interesting. He used to clear the basic ideas by using all sorts of explanations. The tools used by him were only the blackboard and chalk pieces. With the help of these simple tools, he used to present a clear picture before us.

Once it so happened that the students insisted repeatedly that he should dictate a note on a particular topic. He was reluctant. What he did instead was to write out a short note on the notice board for our special reference. This example created a profound impression on my mind and I came to the conclusion that dictation of notes in the classroom was wastage of time. As I understood, the basic purpose of lecturing gets defeated if this method is followed. In any case what are textbooks for if not for further study and reference?

Even though I am not in favour of dictating notes in the classroom, I must confess I have not been able to resist the pressure of my students. Everyone else was doing it and my not doing it created tension, it appeared. Also I noted for myself the example of one other colleague in my college. He refused to dictate notes in the classroom. The students complained against him to the Principal who in turn convinced him to dictate notes in the classroom. It is a well known fact that coaching classes are run and college students crowd them in large numbers. Why? The key to the success of these coaching classes is nothing but the circulation of cyclostyled material.

IV

While explaining the structure of compounds in the classroom, it is necessary for students to imagine a three-dimensional structure. As part of my teaching therefore, I attempted to draw a picture on the blackboard. It so happens that I am basically poor in drawing, and even with a lot of practice at home, I could not draw a particular structure on the blackboard. So much so that sometime students would laugh. This made me nervous. After a number of attempts when I found that I had failed in my particular method of teaching, which was to explain and simultaneously draw the structure on the blackboard, I discontinued that method. Instead I started coming to the class with readymade charts and pre-drawn figures.

As a result of my having to struggle with these difficulties, I came to the conclusion that the use of audiovisual aids was not only helpful but even essential. These aids did the job of explaining in a few minutes what cannot be explained even after several hours of teaching. But these facilities are not available in most colleges. In saying this I am talking of colleges situated in states like Maharashtra. What happens in small and remote places can well be imagined.

In a subject like Chemistry, while explaining topics like atomic structure, molecular structure, chemical bonding, Coordination Chemistry mechanics of reactions etc., a lot of imagination is required. Teachers sometime use models to explain these concepts. But these models are either not easily available or are not available in requisite numbers. My experience as a teacher tells me that if these models and aids are used and the basic concepts are made clear, students feel inspired and motivated to learn more about them. They ask for reference books. Here is an opportunity for a teacher to expose his students to the wider world. They get encouraged to go to the library.

In this connection I cannot help recall one other incident also. I was teaching the structure of complex in Coordination Chemistry. I myself was not all that clear about it but one of my students, while answering questions in the classroom, asked me to clarify my own ideas. When I asked him to prepare a model of this structure he did so and even got a prize in the science exhibition. For anyone to imagine that he does not learn from his students is to make a claim which is not always consistent with one's experience.

Organising science exhibitions creates an occasion to take an initiative both for students and teachers. Sometime students even of average ability also show talent and imagination. When I was a student of the first year degree course, one of my classmates used to take interest only in electrical experiments, so much so that he failed in other subjects in the annual examination. By virtue of his imagination and innovativeness he found a device which automatically cuts off the radio when the programme is finished. If such talents are found in anyone, it is incumbent upon the teacher to nurture them.

In this connection I would like to say that a well-equipped laboratory has an important role in higher education. It is by working in the laboratory that one can get new ideas and experiment creatively.

However this facility is not to be found even in all city colleges. To talk about rural areas would not be realistic therefore. Non-availability of books and insufficient reading facilities are common complaints in colleges in mofusil areas.

In these colleges students come mostly from the rural background, and they are, in most cases, first generation learners. Exceptions apart, not many of them are well-prepared for higher education. It is difficult to make them cultivate the habit of reading and make use of the library and so on. But there is one advantage. Teachers and students can come close to one another, for the place is small and the frequent contact makes it possible for them to come close to one another. Everyone knows everyone. Sometimes there is interaction even between parents and teachers.

In such situations a teacher has to be particularly careful. Everything that he does is noticed by students and indeed by the whole town. In big cities, once the teacher leaves the premises of the college, he is not usually identified as a teacher. People cannot recognise him and he gets lost in the crowd. While in college, students certainly expect him to provide a model but outside the college he is one of the crowd.

During recent years I have noticed a change coming over the younger generation. In this connection I can cite the example of a woman colleague. She used to wear a large number of glass bangles and always made sure that they were of the matching colour. In fact, she was so particular about the matching business that every part of her outfit, including her pen and other appurtenances were of the same colour. In the college therefore she was named as the 'matching lady'.

Nobody could object to the matching business but when she wrote on the blackboard there was a jingling sound and it disturbed the atmosphere in the class. I suggested to her several times indirectly not to wear so many bangles while coming to college. She did not like it nor did she take my advice. In such a situation can we talk about some kind of a code of ethics which in the case of women may also include how they dress?

My experience is that if one has been a teacher for a long time, it begins to show in one's dress and conduct. Sometimes even outsiders can make out that one is a teacher. Travelling in Bombay suburban trains, sometimes people have asked me "Are you a teacher?" Surely something in the manner I carry and conduct myself leads them to ask me such a question.

V

As a teacher one comes across students from different strata of life. While poor students are few and far between, a large number of them come from the middle class; some from the upper middle class and a few of them from very rich families. Each one of them has a different kind of bearing and a different set of values. Those who come from affluent backgrounds move about with confidence but those coming from the lower strata of society, particularly from backward classes, stand out as different from the rest.

In the college where I am working at present, special attention is paid to those coming from backward classes. Some of them are also working students who come from the economically weaker sections of society. The college gives them various facilities such as free books, freeships and sometimes even scholarships. Still I find that these students lag behind.

For example, in the very first year a large number of them who come from the backward sections drop out. Their parents are hardly educated and most of them go about with the feeling of being inferior to the rest. This is disquieting but one does not know what do to in such situations.

A particularly difficult problem is that of the medium of instruction. The medium in city colleges is mostly English. Most of them have been educated through their own languages and it is at the college stage that they switch from one medium to the other. Students in general find it difficult but those coming from the backward classes find it even more difficult.

For days together, they sit through the first term but are not in a position to follow the lectures. No wonder the result at the end of the first terminal examination is usually poor in their case. Even those who score well at the secondary school examination sometimes fail. This leads to loss of self-confidence on their part. Without going into the wider question of the medium of instruction, it is clear that there is a very real problem here and something needs to be done to resolve it.

Sometimes while lecturing in the classroom, we deliver a part of the lecture in English and a part in the student's mother tongue. This helps

Grappling with Problems

to some extent but is not entirely satisfactory. Because of the sense of deprivation from which they suffer, not many of them are bold enough to approach the teacher to solve their difficulties. A few of the more concerned teachers do go out of the way to ask them if they have followed and in what manner they can help them.

But it is not every teacher who does so. Some students therefore always lag behind whereas some are able to overcome hurdles. Despite the fact that various kinds of facilities are given to them such as free accommodation in the hostel and so on, most of them are unable, for instance, to meet the mess bill. One student stands out in my memory. In spite of these odds, he never gave up. During his entire student career spread over four years, he worked in a hospital in the night shift and attended college during the day. This requires strong determination and everyone does not have it.

In such circumstances, students from backward classes have to be helped. Not only is it necessary to provide them with all facilities such as exemption from tuition fee, room rent, even free meals and so on, the more important thing is to help them to develop confidence in themselves. The best way in which this can be done is to help them discover their inherent capacities. Since quite a few of them have these capacities, it is for the college and the teacher working on its behalf whose responsibility it becomes to help them to do so.

Institutions committed to upliftment of backward students are very few. In fact, some colleges do not give them admission except as per requirements of the rules. This is painful. Attitudes towards them have certainly changed over the years but I am sorry to say that this is not happening in institutions which offer professional education, medicine and engineering for example.

To some extent teachers coming from this background also encounter similar difficulties. Though a certain quota of jobs is reserved for them and so on, the attitude is one of patronage as if they were being done a favour and so on. Given a little help and encouragement, some of them shape into good and competent teachers.

VI

As a science teacher, one insistent thought that comes to my mind needs to be expressed. I find that even after they have taken a degree, science students, particularly when they join industry, are not able to perform satisfactorily. Their knowledge is shallow and limited. Industry however is nowadays being modernised at a rapid pace. Sophisticated technologies are being introduced. But we in colleges follow out-dated techniques and do not impart even those to our students effectively.

Clearly, the syllabi need to be modernised. This however would have two other implications. One is that perhaps more expensive equipment would have to be acquired. Therefore funds would have to be provided for this purpose. Secondly, some of the teachers, particularly those who have been teaching for quite some time and are not in touch with the latest in their respective fields would have to be helped so that they are in a position to handle the streamlined syllabi. Living in a city like Bombay, I am particularly aware of the acute need of taking some steps in this direction.

11
Walking on Water

D.N. WAKHLU

SOME persons are born teachers but others stumble into the profession. Mine was a strange journey. As a child living in a large middle class family, I grew in the company of children of two distinct age groups; some of my own age, others a few years younger. Emphasis on learning was a general feature of the household, and my father was particularly charged with the responsibility of children's education in the entire family.

His bedroom in the large family house is called the "Paran Kuth" (the reading room) even today. He had been a founder teacher of the National High School and I often heard his descriptions of his experiences as a teacher. Being somewhat good in my study, the task of coaching my cousins and interacting with them at different levels became a frequent routine for me. In association with an elder cousin of mine, who recently retired as a College Principal, I started a "home school" where we would hold classes, produce plays and even attempted to write books of sorts. The whole family would often be witness to our theatrical performances.

With that background, one day I found myself enrolled as an engineering student in the Banaras Hindu University. India had been free for two years and the nation was jubilant. The mood was vibrant. Jawaharlal Nehru was the great teacher going round every nook and corner of the country, giving long lectures in his inimitable style. The vision of a new India on the threshold of a new beginning was very much before us.

Science and technology offered an opportunity and a challenge. The future looked good and marvellous. And indeed, in a flushed mood, I started off my vocation as a civil engineer in the Irrigation Department of my home state. This provided me with a unique opportunity to meet people in the villages, the common folk who are usually the oppressed ones, as well as their leaders in whom they reposed their trust and confidence.

During this period I allowed the teacher in me to come forth again. In the evenings, my surveying tent would be surrounded by a few villagers eager to know more about the modern world. I enjoyed such chats immensely. Later, I would address audiences in the villages explaining to the people the significance of a particular project that was being undertaken in their area and for their benefit. This was a role which seemed to suit my temperament admirably.

Postgraduate education in engineering in those days was neither common, nor considered necessary. However, just then one such course was announced at Roorkee, and this did the trick. I was bitten by the higher education bug and the name of Roorkee fascinated me. As a child, I had heard so much about Roorkee from the PWD colleagues of my father, that its glamour had stuck. I got admission to this course and with great difficulty, I got relieved from service on leave without pay for higher education. The PWD Minister had to intervene in this routine administrative matter. That is another long story. Within a year I was back at my job, better equipped, with a much wider vision and an enhanced appreciation of the world around me.

I accomplished a number of challenging tasks and, at a comparatively young age, was called upon to shoulder the managerial responsibility of a large and complex establishment in the state, which, in retrospect, I believe I managed quite well. This phase did not, however, last long. Destiny and human caprice intervened and I resigned my job to take up another. This time I landed a teaching assignment at the University of Roorkee. My teaching career of over three decades began there and I have never looked back again.

II

To begin with, I was given the assignment of design classes with students. In such situations there is close contact between the teacher and the students. There was very little of formal lecturing and I enjoyed passing on to my students the experience I had had and took pains to explain the practical aspects of a civil engineer's work. The students I taught were a highly motivated group and of high calibre.

There were very few problems in respect of student discipline or their attitude to work. During these early days, I discovered a strange difference in the work ethos of the teacher and the practising engineer. The working engineer is used to long hours of work in his office or on the job in the field. As a teacher, I found myself suddenly left alone to plan, guide, and monitor my own work. I could think of no teachers I could model myself on and no training in pedagogy was either given or was available. I decided that the best way to influence my students was to be engaged in engineering study and related work myself. It occurred to me that the lax ways of the typical teacher would be detrimental to my own growth as well as bad for the impact I would make on the students. Therefore, while supervising routine work of the students, I would busy myself with related engineering work in the same hall. This provided the students with an example and produced the needed enthusiasm amongst them. I cannot recall any situation in which I encountered self doubt or embarrassment vis-a-vis my job in hand.

By and large the students seemed satisfied with my guidance and supervision. I learnt a lot more about the ways of teachers and universities in this first encounter. That experience and knowledge was new. With zeal and enthusiasm, I also took part in the administrative and planning tasks which helped in my future development and also my role as an engineering teacher.

With this first encounter behind me, I took up another teaching assignment at Banaras Hindu University. Here I lectured to students as well as supervised their design work. The lecturing in my own field of specialization provided me with an opportunity to devise new ways of teaching. I believed that my field experience was useful in relating the subject matter to real life situations. A great deal of student interest in a subject is related to his perception of its utility to the practical field of work. The students I taught in those days were usually of middle class origin but with high motivation and good basic ability. There was indeed no communication gap. Norms and traditions had been well established over a long period of time and these were not challenged.

I tried my utmost to do my assignments with zeal, attempting all the time to come upto the expectations of my senior colleagues, some of whom had been my most distinguished teachers in my earlier career. This spurred me on, and my students were equally enthused. What distressed me during this period was not any adverse observation of student behaviour but the goings on in the university and the teaching faculty. There were sharp differences of opinion on educational management and a lot of group rivalry stemming essentially from the stresses caused by new developments under the Five-Year Plan projects.

I reflected on these matters and came to the conclusion that an improved style of management in order to achieve better academic ethos would go a long way in improving the contents as well as the quality of education. Constraints in the way of new experiments were many, yet it was possible to go along the traditional ways with modifications here and there in the light of one's own thinking and experience.

It is at this time that I formulated my belief in "revolution and compromise" as the cornerstone of my conduct as a teacher. In a social milieu like ours, it appeared hazardous to bring about too drastic a change too rapidly. This was consistent with the general approach to everything that was being attempted in the country at that time. The students seemed to be satisfied with this approach as well, and I did not encounter any difficulty with them.

It was a pleasure to go visiting industrial establishments with the students. Teamwork with discipline prevailed all throughout. I also did a three-week stint with senior students on a project assignment in the open fields at Ranchi, Bihar. The experience was rewarding and all of us loved the assignment immensely.

Contrary to my adverse experience with students in recent years about which I shall talk later, there was not a single incident I can recall which arose from student mischief, idiosyncracy, or any inconvenience felt by them in respect of food or camping facilities. I am emphasizing this point because it has got a lot to do with students' upbringing and motivation which, on present day reckoning, have become a total casualty in the educational system.

III

These early experiences as a teacher were my formative years in the profession. Some great examples of teachers were before me. I soon realized that ideally the teacher in engineering must possess three basic attributes, namely communication skill, creative imagination, and uptodate technical know-how in his subject. He must be abreast of the latest in his field and keep himself engaged in research and consultancy work on real life problems.

I was fortunate to have before me some fine examples of teachers who had combined these roles admirably in their professional activities as teachers. My efforts as a teacher were throughout confined to two compartments, namely communication with the students in the classroom and the laboratory; and work towards self improvement. This two-pronged approach to my profession has remained with me as a constant feature.

Laboratory work in engineering courses is part of the curriculum. As a student, I was trained to attach considerable importance to every aspect of work in the laboratory so much so that we were expected to complete the given assignment with sketches and graphs during a continuous three hour stint exactly in the same atmosphere as one would have in a working laboratory.

My experience as a teacher however, brought to my attention the fact that many students were not creatively involved in such exercises and, therefore, did not take the fullest advantage of such assignments. Therefore, I approached this task differently. Instead of giving the students the task of doing a routine and standard experiment on a particular set-up, I would ask them to play around with the apparatus, let water flow and see carefully what all they observed, report faithfully, and gradually approach the problem ensuring meanwhile that the various measurements were taken and all preliminaries attended to.

Such an attitude roused genuine curiosity in the students to know more about many observed phenomena and thereby seek to learn more about them from books and literature. The experimental approach thus became more meaningful for the students. Constant effort was, however, needed to maintain the sagging student interest in laboratory work.

It dawned on me that the best pedagogical approach to training students professionally would only slightly help the students unless they had aptitude and motivation whereas the better calibre student with aptitude and motivation would be definitely trained better in an innovative teaching atmosphere. The former type of student puts the teacher's devotion to a severe test, whereas the better student provides him solace and creative satisfaction so that the torch is kept lighted and improved steadily.

This faith has sustained me in my profession even at the worst of times. No matter what the constraints, my attempt has always been to give the best to the students, even while it was obvious that there was reluctance, nay even irreverence, in the student mind for reasons beyond the teacher's control.

Laboratory work also suffered for another reason. Many laboratories were not well set up. I was fortunate to get an opportunity to build a new laboratory from scratch. This work gave me a good opportunity to share the experience with the students and make them feel part of the team as engineer trainees. I used such opportunities throughout my teaching career. I would invariably share the work with students and use real life examples as often as possible to demonstrate to them the usefulness of the experimental method.

The course of my own growth was set in a strange way by my inner drive and the remnants of childhood impressions. As a child I was exposed to the ritual of daily prayers. Voracious reading of books was another family trait acquired automatically and, finally, I had developed considerable interest in personal psychology as well as the rudiments of Communism.

All these amorphous ideas and prejudices arising therefrom were to be shaped in the atmosphere of the professional college in a city of famous traditions. Changes did take place to put my life and my thinking on a new track. But I vividly recall one book which opened my eyes to a new approach to life and which set me on my professional track. This was *Executive Thinking and Action* by De Armond published by McGraw Hill. Managing myself, managing my tasks, planning my life became for me the hall-marks of a truly professional career.

As a teacher I therefore attempted to provide my engineering trainees sufficient motivation to understand their professional life in its totality and relate the various subjects of study to the final goal of becoming creative persons with an ability to design and create engineered systems for the benefit of man keeping always in mind the three cardinal principles of engineering design namely, economy, safety and beauty.

I had missed this approach so much in my student days that I became obsessed with the idea of giving sufficient exposure to the professional aspects of their work. I sincerely believed then, and I am confirmed in this belief now, that a student who is not trained with this basic awareness remains at best a good technician and he does not give his best to society as a professional engineer.

I devised and began to teach a course on Works Management for Civil Engineers which was well taken by the students. There was a lot of interest and liveliness in discussions and the professional aspects became relevant in their totality. Over the years I have continued to teach management to my students and always impressed on them the need to balance in their mental make-up the three essential components that go to make the professional engineer viz. technical and scientific knowledge, social awareness and communication skill.

As a teacher, I believed that higher research skills and a Ph.D. were necessary for progress in my career. I was happy to get the opportunity for such work at Birmingham, England. This was another opportunity of seeing teachers and students at close quarters in a different milieu. The contrasts were many. I was specially struck by the maturity of the young students.

This was a period of reflection and introspection for me. I was being groomed to become a better teacher, so I tried to acquire all that I thought was good for my country and for my students in the years to come. The contrasts in efficiency and management of academic affairs were too obvious. The number of students was insignificant as compared to the hordes of students back home. This prompted me to seek answers to our problems and reflect on ways and means of achieving the same.

What bothered me, and still does, is the absence of real creative talent in us. It is a puzzle to me why, given the same brain power and intellectual endowment, we, in India, are not able to produce the talent which is otherwise nurtured in foreign universities and from the same human material.

IV

With my renewed enthusiasm, I resumed my teaching work in a newly established professional college. We had to teach in temporary classrooms and makeshift laboratories. Enthusiasm was high and the students of the first batch of entrants were setting a good example in respect of building up traditions of hard work and doing good engineering assignments in the laboratory as well as the design hall. The constraints of inadequate infrastructure in respect of laboratories and classrooms hampered our maintaining high standards, but this was offset by the fact that the enthusiasm of the teachers and students was quite high and the latter were highly motivated. They were helpful in appreciating the teachers' role and did more than their share of work to set before them higher standards of achievement.

It was during this period that I got myself associated with professional bodies like the Institution of Engineers (India) and the American Society of Civil Engineers which provided me sufficient literature in my own speciality as well as in respect of general professional development. This gave me many ideas to share with my students. Obviously, this association must have also shaped my approach to teaching in the classroom and my attitude as a professional engineer. I would often tell my students that the hallmarks of a good professional engineer are (i) creative thinking, (ii) dedicated work, and (iii) excellent deportment. I sincerely felt that if I could constantly motivate the students to improve themselves in these directions, it would be in their and the society's best interest.

The late sixties were a turbulent period in the country's history and student unrest became quite widespread. In the past, students' unrest was unheard of in professional institutions. However, now we had our share of problems in the engineering colleges as well. I discovered that my task as a teacher was no more confined to training students in professional engineering only, but also to train them in basic human values. Indeed in many cases we had to train them more to be good human beings than to be good students so that they could join the mainstream of the country as professional engineers and not merely as rough hewn technicians. They must be matured and well educated persons, I insisted.

Political overtones were evident in the way the students' problems were projected. There were extraneous elements which were constantly interfering with the smooth functioning of academic work. I vividly recollect one Vice-Chancellor saying, *"Teaching today is the most difficult task and it is like walking on water."* The problems of student unrest arose due to many reasons: the number of students was large and human contact at the personal level was often well nigh impossible; students came from varied background and so on. I had the Vice-Chancellor's son and the sweeper's son next door in the same classroom. They have near equal IQ's, but possess vastly different perceptions about their past, present and future; even personal habits were different, often varying around divergent extremes.

I was alive to these difficulties and apprehensions in the students' mind. Often these arose out of these situations and many others. Sometimes they were fuelled by an input of extraneous socio-political considerations. I showed a lot of patience in handling excited and misguided students. It was absolutely necessary to create an atmosphere of near total impartiality and have an objective judgement in academic, administrative and personal matters. This has not been an easy task. I had to learn as much from the students as I had to give them in return.

I recall two examples of such interactions which will highlight the importance of the teacher's role in educating the students properly. I was lecturing to a class of about seventy senior students on the topic of Fluid Mechanics. Just a few minutes after the lecture had begun, and while I was writing on the black-board, some student threw an egg which crashed on the black-board but fell a few paces away from where I was standing. The egg yolk did not fall on me, but I was taken aback.

This was the first time in my long teaching career of about twenty years that such a thing had happened in my classroom. I stopped lecturing but did not leave the classroom in a huff, as many teachers are prone to do in such a situation. I tried to find out the student who had done the mischief and assured him of forgiveness if he were to own up his action. Nobody responded. I told the students why such an action was disgraceful for a professional engineer. They listened to me in pindrop silence.

After the lecture I went to my staff room and forgot about the matter. Next day I took a lecture on the same topic with the same class without any further problems. This came as a complete surprise to many students; they had expected me to strike my work as protest against their misbehaviour. This action of mine would give them cause for a strike and disruption of academic life at the behest of some instigators who did not want peace on the campus.

Quite often, I used to take time off from lectures and explain to students why they should not allow themselves to be treated as mere cogs in the wheel and misused for nefarious ends. I believe this had its impact on a large number of them but there was a small minority which did not heed such advice because they were influenced by other teachers for reasons one cannot go into. Often these teachers had different expectations from their students and their motives were not necessarily connected with students' training and professional needs.

On another occasion, the college teachers had boarded the staff bus to depart for their residences at the end of the day. Some mischievous students forcibly entered the bus without permission and started arguing with their teachers. There was exchange of hot words and some students used abusive language against the teachers. I was sitting somewhere in the front row and found the situation intolerable. I tried to plead with the students to behave themselves but they did not heed my advice. Thereupon, I promptly left the bus and walked to my home on foot, a distance of 11 kms from the college. This action was spontaneous and might have had its impact on the students.

Next morning when I reached college, the teachers had gone on strike, protesting against the behaviour of the students. I requested my colleagues not to adopt such a unprofessional attitude, because it may have an adverse impact on students. I sincerely believed then, as I do now, that any hostile confrontation between students and teachers is detrimental to the cultivation of a conducive academic ethos in our temples of learning.

V

As a teacher, I have always found it extremely difficult to maintain a balance between my mandate in the task of communicating engineering know-how to students on the one hand, and interacting with students as human beings on the other. They need a lot of grooming in a hundred different ways to enable them to discharge their responsibilities as good citizens and become good engineers after graduation. Difficult as this task may be, the balance has to be constantly maintained.

In this respect a personal example is the best example; students learn best in this way. That is why I have always maintained a flexible attitude as a teacher. This does not, however, mean a compromising attitude in respect of basic principles. What it means is possessing an openness of mind which prepares us to listen to and appreciate another point of view as much as our own.

Our society—particularly after the revolutionary changes that have occurred after independence—is a dynamic and changing society, struggling to establish a new system of values which are truly in harmony with our cherished goals of socialism, democracy and secularism. In our plural society this task is yet to be achieved. What is more, this has to be a continuous process. The teacher should have a constant awareness of the social reality and tailor his approach to teaching and academic work with the utmost of sensitivity, independence, and objective judgement in respect of all situations that might arise from time to time.

Our examination system of the by-gone days is a relic of the past which harasses the creative teacher as well as the student without much profit. I have often said that, the presence of the *sealing wax culture* in the universities is the greatest bane we have inherited from the past. Although I have failed to have a better system available to me, my evaluation of students' work has always been carried out with the intention of getting the best out of them rather than discourage them by highlighting manifold faults only.

A human being is very complex, and a student even much more so. I have never been able to condemn even the worst of students without misgivings in my mind. I have always found, on a deeper probe and better interaction with them, that even the worst human being has talents and qualities that could be improved and nurtured with patience, firmness and love.

12

Scattering the Seeds

MADHU KISHWAR

THE decision to be a teacher is one of the most rational decisions I have made and I have never regretted it. The main reason for my choice of this profession was that, of the various professions open to me, it offered the most freedom. As a teacher, one is relatively less tyrannised over by authority. Likewise, as a teacher one has relatively less power over others. In most other jobs and professions, one does not have a relationship of equality with one's co-workers. They are placed either above or below one. However, in the teaching profession one is placed on an equal footing vis-a-vis one's colleagues except maybe for the principal. Even senior colleagues do not have any special powers over junior colleagues.

The maximum power one has over students is the power to have them penalised for not coming to class. Since a fresh batch of students arrives each year, one cannot get stuck with one set of hierarchical relationships. The fluid situation offers the teacher the opportunity to grow.

Many of my friends have gone into the civil services and into private sector jobs. Most people consider teaching a relatively low paid, low status profession. For women, it is considered suitable because it permits them to put more time and energy into looking after the husband and children. Marriage was not on my agenda, but active involvement in various social and political issues certainly was. As a teacher, one is not forbidden to participate in such activities. As a government employee, one has to tread very carefully for fear of being stopped by the authorities.

II

Another important reason I chose to teach is that teaching is based on interaction with human beings. The primary concern of a teacher is not with files and papers, orders and permissions, as is that of an official in a public or private sector undertaking.

I teach in a coeducational, non-elite, off campus college in Delhi. I prefer it to women's colleges, because the atmosphere in women's institutions is far more tyrannical. Principals in women's colleges are more authoritarian vis-a-vis the staff and students; teachers too tyrannise over students more thoroughly. However, in mixed colleges, the atmosphere tends to be more relaxed and more liberal because men do not allow themselves to be bullied as much as women do.

Being a woman teacher in a mixed college does have some disadvantages. As a group, women play a peripheral role in college affairs. Male colleagues take over the running of the college as if it was their natural prerogative, and leave space only for a token woman or two. The same is true for women students, especially if they happen to be in a minority, as in my college. Both women students and teachers tend to be inhibited and self-conscious. The few who are not so inclined stick out like a sore thumb and are made targets of gossip and slander. The atmosphere of the college is so male oriented and male defined that there is little place in it for any creative functioning by women.

In my college, most students have very low language skills and next to no competence in conceptualising. Their abilities have been systematically damaged by 12 years of our current brand of schooling. I am supposed to teach them English literature, but most of them cannot write a simple sentence in correct English, nor are they fluent in writing in their own mother tongue—Hindi or Punjabi.

In such a situation, it is very easy to develop contempt for the students and become totally cynical. The students' lack of abilities can be misconstrued as a confirmation of the presumed intellectual abilities of even the stupidest of teachers. The teacher's inability to communicate can easily be explained away as the students' dullness.

Another convenient way of dealing with the dilemma is to stop at blaming the system for the communication gap, while abdicating all responsibility to communicate. While it is undeniable that the system is largely responsible for both the students' and the teachers' predicament, a more systemic way of thinking should helps us develop greater empathy.

I tell myself that it is unlikely I can do my students great good. However, I should ensure that I do the least possible harm. They should not leave my classroom worse off than when they entered it.

III

The first thing I had to do was to shed the illusion that I could inculcate in them an appreciation of great literature, or even impart the skills of language. It is unlikely that those who graduate will ever be able to write a letter in correct English. Although I did try to encourage them to keep a diary and to read books, this was an uphill task. They have little access to books, and more important, few of them have any tradition of reading or writing in their families.

I decided that my primary role was not to instil a love of reading and writing, nor to help them get good marks. I warn them that I am not likely to be very successful in helping them get grand results. That would require helping them acquire the techniques of being good examinees, or learning by heart, and using guide books intelligently.

Instead, I try to present my students with a vision of a life that is not confined to stereotyped channels, a life that is more than getting 50 per cent marks, getting a secure job, joining the family business, marrying and producing children. I want to show them that other possibilities also exist in life, that some people actually live with other aspirations.

Secondly, I try to encourage their curiosity about their world and to stimulate an ability to ask relevant questions about anything and everything in it. I cannot boast of any great success in this because their environment, including their university education, is geared to repress this way of thinking.

Thirdly, I try to encourage them to take responsibility for their own actions, to act on their own initiative without any orders from anyone. I cannot do this unless I am also willing to let go of authority. The system of compulsory attendance in our university system is the most visible sign of students' passivity. They have to sit in the class even if they are bored to death.

I inform the students that I will not use the attendance system to tyrannise over them. Each day, after taking the roll call, I say that anyone who wants to leave the class is free to do so. At first, they could not believe that I meant it seriously. Even those who wanted to leave were afraid to do so, lest I turn vindictive towards them or report them to the principal. They wanted to cut classes but did not have the courage to take the moral responsibility for it by doing it openly.

Gradually, as they realised that I was serious, some of them began to leave. This also meant testing myself. Once, when the whole class got up and left, I did not know how to take it. I told myself that I should not see this as an attack on me, but as a sign that they were taking seriously what I had said. The next day, they all stayed on in class.

On the other hand, I insist that they take responsibility for cutting classes in the sense that they come for the roll call and leave only after that. Some students did not show up throughout the year but came at the end to ask me to give them attendance for the year. I refused to do this. I told them that if they did not want to come even for the roll call, they must give in writing that they were not willing even to step into class. That would involve taking some responsibility for their actions. To come like a coward at the end of the term is moral laziness and an act of evasion.

IV

All these experiments involved many risks for me. For instance, the fact that I do not try to look like or behave like the authority figure a teacher is expected to be creates uncertainties in the minds of the students. I was the first woman teacher in the college not to wear a sari and to ride a motor bike. I also talked freely with the students and could easily be mistaken for one of them. I was one of the few English teachers who enjoyed teaching English literature in Hindi because that ensured that the students at least understood what I said.

I make special efforts to get the students to talk in the class which is usually not encouraged. Not knowing how to comprehend all this, some students would try to act smart, and test me out by talking disrespectfully or even by letting off crackers in class, or sending pigeons flying in through the windows. I had to learn not to react in a disciplinarian manner by scolding them or trying to devastate them with sarcasm. I had to learn to laugh with them, to get them to understand that respect and fear are not synonymous and to see the distinction between them is the beginning of liberal education.

Another experiment is with writing assignments. I correct their assignments but do not give marks or grades. It is very hard for them to accept this, to understand that an essay can be evaluated by its own strengths and weaknesses, not necessarily by marks that measure it against others' essays.

Also, instead of asking questions regarding the text, the answers to which they would usually copy from guidebooks in preparation for their examinations, I ask them to write about themselves or about a film they have seen. Sometimes, I take a class to see a film, and then ask them to write about it. The idea of seeing a film together gets them very excited. Many girls say their parents will not allow them to go to see a film. Sometimes, I have to write letters to each parent before they get permission.

Further, some girls are themselves wary of going to a film in the company of boys lest the boys tease them later. This generates a lot of discussion in the class. What kind of confidence are male students able to engender in their female classmates, if the latter are not willing to go to a film with them in a group?

In a mixed class where girls are in a minority, they tend to be very inhibited. When I ask a question, a boy will answer almost each time. I have to make a very special effort to get girls to speak, address them individually, and forbid boys to interrupt. This could mean waiting in silence for 10 minutes before the girl works up the confidence to say a word.

Encouraging freer interaction between boys and girls can be easily misinterpreted and get both them and me into difficulties. To give an instance. Some years ago, two of my students—a boy and a girl—came literally crying to me, saying their identity cards had been confiscated by the office staff. They were too afraid and embarrassed to tell me why. I went and asked the person who had viciously scolded them and confiscated their identity cards. His response was angry and hysterical: "Madam, you had better not interfere. You can't imagine what I caught them doing on the terrace."

Given the fact that the terrace he mentioned is not a lonely place and usually bunches of students hang around there, I could not imagine that their offence could possibly have been any more than holding hands or, at the very most, hugging or kissing. I repeatedly kept asking him what exactly they had done. All I got in response was a long lecture on declining standards of mortality. Neither he nor others who intervened would tell me what the offence was.

The two students were in a state of panic because the staff had threatened to inform their parents. When I tried to plead for them, some of my colleagues were outraged and yelled at me: "What do you want to make of this college—a brothel? Do you want us to keep beds in the classrooms so that they can have free sex any time they like?"

Now, I am no advocate of surreptitious hugs and kisses in college corridors but I was disturbed to see that the same persons who were so outraged at this "obscene" behaviour would not have been half as deeply disturbed if two male students had stabbed each other with knives or split each other's skulls with stones or bricks or burnt a couple of buses for fun. Such episodes happen not infrequently and are treated as more or less routine.

A couple more of such interventions on my part, and I would have been branded a bad influence on students, if not an outright "loose" woman.

V

While teaching literature, there is great scope to relate the issue raised to the issues of our society and our lives. Some students even read *Manushi* on their own initiative, after coming to know of my involvement with it, though I never try to push it down their throats.

All this is a very slow process and a hard struggle. The prescribed syllabus has also to be completed. There are many other obstacles. I am more and more aware of the limitations of trying to influence students' thinking. I have become relatively more modest on this score. If one becomes intoxicated with the idea of influencing students' ways of thinking, one can do a lot of damage to oneself and to them. One can end up feeling frustrated and contemptuous of those who fail to live up to one's expectations.

The teacher's role is to scatter the seeds. Two may sprout or two hundred. One cannot be sure of what will happen, if anything; but one should not despair.

VI

One illusion I had to shed was the temptation to see myself as a role model. Role models may be relevant in situations where the students have meaningful options available to them or the freedom to mould their lives according to their aspirations.

Most of my students come from very poor quality government schools. They are painfully self conscious about their lack of skills and academic ability. As a result, very few aspire to do well in studies and even fewer have any illusions about being able to enter grand professions. Most of them are resigned to the course of life predetermined by their family circumstances.

Almost all the girl students are sent to college to qualify for the marriage market wherein even lower middle class boys today demand graduate brides. In most cases, their families will not allow them to take up jobs. Consequently, very few of them see much purpose in serious or systematic study.

If I try to get them to take their studies seriously, I have inevitably to encourage them to revolt against their families. That is a very risky path, given the crippling ways in which most women in our country are kept dependent on their families. Apart from my own dilemma about whether or not to urge girl students to take this risky path, most of them are acutely aware that even if they do attempt defiance, they cannot go very far on their own steam, given their limited skills and resources. It is unlikely that many of them can even get an ordinary clerical job on their own strength.

It is not very different for male students except that, apart from matrimony, their families have other plans for them. The sons of petty shopkeepers and businessmen are expected to join their fathers' enterprise. The few who have to take up jobs are likely to get no more than low level clerical or sales jobs where pulling of strings is likely to be more needed than educational qualifications alone. Hence, very few come motivated for studies. Even those who do can rarely retain their interest because the syllabi structures and content are so mindlessly foolish.

Thus, over the years, I have found that, while at the human level, I could easily build a good equation with a number of my students, only a very small number could be inspired into taking themselves more seriously. These few are usually those whose families allow them some minimal space for independent decision making.

The prerequisite for a good human equation was that I shed most of my grand ideas about "inspiring" students into great achievements.

Over the years, an empathic understanding of the unenviable predicament of most of my students helped me accept the limitations of my own role as a teacher within the given situation and prevented me from becoming a frustrated cynic.

Teaching has taught me a lot. I have learnt to try and communicate fairly complex ideas in the simplest ways possible, for example, to discuss Shaw, offering some comparisons with an Amitabh film, while, at the same time, trying not to lose the spirit of Shaw.

In many senses, I have remained a student. I have kept working for other degrees while teaching, And, with *Manushi*, one has to be a perpetual student. Teaching and learning, I see myself as trying to enhance both my own and others' freedom, in however small a way.

13
Teaching as Provocation

UPENDRA BAXI

THERE are probably as many conceptions and practices of teaching as there are teachers. To teach is to take part in the tradition of teaching; and the tradition offers both constraints and opportunities to its ever-increasing constituents. If the tradition offers a spiritual home to some, to others it constitutes a set of provocations. But paradoxically it is only against the backdrop of a taught tradition of teaching that one may be a rebel!

The tradition defines 'teaching' and provides means of distinguishing between 'good' and 'bad' teaching. Just as literary theory creates and sustains models of 'classics.' But as with literary theory, so with educational theory, what we should not miss is the simple fact that dominant conceptions of 'teaching' (like 'literature') are bound up with ideologies in service of power. Unless, therefore our rigorous self-reflection is available, the rich diversity and individual autonomy of teachers remain only an appearance of freedom within the framework of necessity imposed by traditions.

To the question, "What does one really do when one teaches?" there are, of course, the familiar answers. Answers which tell us, for example, that teaching is

—an *entrepreneurial process* in which aggregates of intellectual (scientific) capital and labour produce systematic transmission of knowledge from the teacher to the taught;

—a *partnership process* wherein the teacher and the taught learn together in asymmetrical ways;

—an *enabling process* in which teaching is regarded as an activity consisting in helping others to learn;

—an *ideological process* where the practice of teaching, and theories about teaching, are either supportive or subversive of patterns of dominant power;

Teaching as Provocation

—a *missionary process* envisaging teachers as evangelists of knowledge and proselytisers of rationality, conceiving teaching as a vocation;

—a *mercenary process* conceiving teaching as a mode of production of exchange-values of knowledge addressed to the creation of income, and the means of income, sufficient to meet the hazards of ever growing material needs and the demands of unconscionable sociability (e.g., teaching stints overseas to provide for dowry payments for Professor's "double-graduate" daughters);

—a *professional process* in which certain knowledge-jobs and cognitive tasks have to be routinely performed as in any other profession.

These seven images of 'teaching' do not, of course, provide even a glimpse of a whole range of other notions of teaching. These include, for example, teaching career as a background to or means of

—pursuing of administrative or trade union career paths at campus and national levels;

—social mobility, especially for the scheduled castes and tribes and other disadvantaged stratas and classes;

—organized assertion of gender equality;

—pursuit of other mid-life passages such as leadership roles in national, educational, research or scientific organizations, policy-planning, United Nations systems assignments;

—ex-officio credibility in public and political life (just note how so many politicians flaunt their 'professorship').

These—and associated uses, symbolic and instrumental—of teaching careers certainly affect, in major and minor ways, current theories and the practice of teaching. They must also affect somewhat social and political development. They cannot, therefore, be ignored. But in what follows I look upon teaching as a set of processes and practices which a group of people commonly called 'teachers' engage in for a substantial portion of their thinking lives. And to my mind these seven images capture, in myriad ways, the traditions of teaching which provide both constraints and opportunities, as the case may be, to the future entrants to teaching.

But, first, let me begin with a retrospection on myself as a 'teacher.'

II

These seven images of teaching did not emerge to consciousness when I first began teaching in the late sixties at the Sydney Law School's Department of Jurisprudence and International Law. The lamented Professor Julius Stone, a renowned authority in both these frontier fields of legal learning, was among the foremost practitioners of the model of teaching as an entrepreneurial process. He believed that the classroom must be the site for transmission of knowledge in all its evolutionary complexity and contradiction.

This required not just the mastery of fields of knowledge but an enormous preparation for each class. He was simply unapproachable for hours before his class; as one saw him go to the classroom one found him as full of nervous tension, after thirty years of teaching, as a novitiate teacher! For him, each class was an occasion to update a section in an encyclopaedia of knowledge; each dialogue in the classroom was a starting point for reformulation and research.

Now this great teacher is no more; and all we have left are a few scattered memories. A couple of generations hence only his books will remain; not his face or voice. Somehow we have all accepted the distinction between the 'oral' and the 'written'; teaching perishes with the teacher, whereas the corpus of writings survives. In a sense, as Jacques Derrida said in a different context, writing is a "carrier of death" signifying the absence of the speaker.

Teaching, in the profoundest sense of the word, has always appeared to me to be *sacrificial*, a process in which the best articulation of personality is achieved in the least lasting form, a process in which the teacher herself is, as it were, fire at the altar of knowledge.

From the first years of teaching in my life at Sydney I learnt less sublime truths, too. I learnt that teaching requires a profound inversion of roles: the teacher has to be taught and the taught in turn teaches something to the teacher, the receivers of knowledge are the givers and the givers are the receivers. Large graduate classes, all oriented towards the career of legal practice, always asked me, by their very existence, two leading questions: "What are you good for in the long run? And what good can you do for us here and now?" The collective presence of the class, even today, in itself constitutes this interrogation.

Teaching as Provocation

Try however I might, I could not answer these questions by redoubtable displays of erudition in the classroom. The second question I began to answer first. The good I can do for you, I said to myself and still say, is to try and address the problems of a future which is not yet impregnated with knowledge that was gathered in a past which was not mine. To me this is the central problematic of all pedagogy and one which requires the utmost fierce integrity to keep in view.

The "past which was not mine" is no idle turn of phrase. There is simply no way, for example, in which I can successfully communicate the transaction of discourse on natural law in the Catholic tradition from Thomas Aquinas and Dunus Scotus. It took me years of empathy, not just erudition, to enter the spirt of theological tradition of Christianity and years as well as to grasp Abu Hanifa's crucial distinction between murder and culpable homicide not turning upon the intention, as in modern law, but on the method of causing death or the justifications of slavery in Aristotle or untouchability in Manu. In ways I cannot articulate here, even when it possesses more than fugitively haunting relevance, I cannot make their past mine.

III

Nor indeed can I possibly make my students' future my own. The present which I share with them prefigures somewhat their future, but I am already obsolescent. Try how hard I might, I simply cannot grasp modern 'rationality' which discourses the safety of nuclear weapons or the inevitability of some 'costs' entailed in experimentation with new forms of life, in the creation and reckless proliferation of lethally hazardous chemical substances. And the world of the future is the world of irreversible advances in science and technology which will fundamentally alter in ways which I can vaguely imagine, the very conception of life and nature through the ongoing cybernetic and biotechnology revolutions.

As a teacher, I constitute the site of articulation of both a past and a future which are not my own to an audience for whom the present is merely a prologue to future they will live or endure as a daily reality. To the question: "What good can you do for us?" my inchoate answer has been to offer a critique of the past and the future, with equally tenuous grounding in both. I wish for a greater coherence in my approach but it has so far eluded me.

I have found it relatively easier to answer the first question, as it turns out. To this question: "What are you good for?" I say: "Do not merely look at what I say; look at what I do with what I say." I simply cannot carry conviction about what I say to young minds unless they see that I mean what I say about the rule of law, human rights, human dignity.

It is this question which led me to struggle successfully for a course on law and aborigines at Sydney in the face of entirely comprehensible faculty opposition. It is the search for an answer to this question that has led me to bouts of social and legal activism in India, in many a context, outside the classroom. Students constitute a jury every year which determines whether a teacher is guilty or not guilty of treating knowledge as a Brahaminic preserve or using it, outside and inside the classroom, as a sword, as a hoe, as a broom, the badges of inferiority of all other *varnas*.

To my mind, teaching and learning are acts of social intervention and they are complete when knowledge accumulated the erudite way is enriched by knowledge earned through encounters which interrogate tyranny, injustice and exploitation enacted before our own eyes even as we 'teach' and 'learn'.

This is a position which carries enormous strains: it dislocates received frameworks of scholarship and science, confuses bounds of relevance, disrupts agendas of scientific work, demands accountability, in most excruciating forms, to the classroom and the society and finally (without being exhaustive) exposes you to a nagging feeling that one is not really good at any thing. I for one certainly wish that I had found some other way of answering this first question. But it is too late for me now to start all over again.

The silent pressure of these questions has made me learn the truth which Paul de Mann celebrated through the phrase: "dialectics of blindness and insight." Even as I felt I was 'transmitting' knowledge, I realized that I was the carrier of mighty nescience in so many ways; what I do not know is far greater than what, at any given point of time, I can justly claim to know. Very early on, I developed an approach to teaching as a *confessional activity*. Every time I bite at the fruit of knowledge, I have to say, I realize the core of my ignorance.

Wrestling with this truth, I learnt yet another: specialization is a way of negating teaching as a confessional activity. Producing its own brands of certitude, specialization reinforces the authority of the knowledge makers and givers. At the more basic level, it constitutes a very special kind of response to one's scholarly finitude; if one may not take all knowledge as one's province, may we not make our *province* as constituting *all* knowledge?

In a confused and confusing way, I have sought fulfilment as a teacher by avoiding any claims to specialization, by always being engaged in encounters with the unfamiliar. The 'taught tradition of teaching' suggests that I must be comprehensively wrong.

The 'taught' tradition of teaching projects powerfully the message that teaching should be a *rational*, never a *hedonistic* process or activity. There exist deep differences between 'rationalist' and 'hedonistic' approaches on every single dimension: knowledge, pedagogy or ideology.

The 'rationalist' standpoint regards knowledge primarily as a set of exchange values: the hedonist primarily as a set of 'use-values'. The 'rationalist' approach demands disciplinary loyalties; the 'hedonist' thrives on riots of multi-disciplinary sensibilities. The 'rationalist' stresses the 'objective', the indeterminacies and pluralities of knowing and knowledges. For the hedonist knowledges are (to use Stanely Fish's striking metaphor) "self-consuming artefacts."

Hedonistic teaching seeks no escape from one's scholarly finitude; rationalist teaching conceives teachers as beings tinged with the infinity of knowledge they bear and create. While rationalist teacher speaks the language of 'reason', her hedonistic colleague affirms the "passion for teaching." For her, teaching, or to put it differently, creative communication in and out of classroom, is a lifelong and lively mission; for the rationalist, teaching is just one of the many modes of creating and sharing knowledge, and compared with research and publication often a subsidiary mode. The 'rationalist' affirms the weight of erudition: the 'hedonist' iterates the joy of reaching out other minds through interpersonal communication and dialogue.

The endowment that the rationalist approach seeks to create is 'tough' minds, capable of wrestling with real life problems in a distinctly disciplinarian mould. The 'hedonist' seeks to create a "soft" training of the mind and inculcates a "soft" awareness of the multidimensionality of life's problems. If for the 'rationalist' the definition of the problem is the beginning of an ordered enquiry and its 'solution' its terminus, for the 'hedonist' the definition of the definitions is a problem and every solution appears as a disguised problem.

In terms of pedagogy, the rationalist teacher tends to sift the "bright" from the "blighted" students, while the 'hedonist' tends to maintain a community of learners. For the 'hedonist', students are more than units of cognition; they are rather full, whole individuals with life histories and futures. The teacher is no *guru* possessed of charisma of knowledge; but an equally bewildered companion and friend. The classroom is the site of collective ecstasies and catharses, essentially therapeutic for both the teacher and the taught. For rationalist teacher, the teacher-taught relationships are principally cognitive, not personal. There are no hurts, no joys; rather orderly exchanges of knowledge through performance of tolerably well-defined roles which structure appropriate social distances and alienations.

The teacher-taught relation here is especially a disembodied one, a relationship between the 'producers' and 'consumers' of knowledge. Bonds of sharing so conspicuous among the 'hedonist' teacher-taught relationships are seen as threatening with anarchy the manicured gardens of ideas in the rationalist processes of 'teaching'.

The hedonistic conception of teaching leads to the politics of commitment to causes; the rationalist conception tends to maintain a respectable, and safe, distance between knowledge and 'politics' of action. If the hedonist, acerbically, accuses the rationalist colleague of sublimating her lust for power through scholarship. the 'rationalist' condemns the hedonist doing propaganda and politics from the sanctuary of superannuated tenures.

The hedonist regards extra and co-curricular activities as integral aspects of teaching and learning: and for some amongst them, extended coffee-table conversations on life, letters and politics are as important as classroom teaching. For the rationalist, the latter is forbidden almost totally; the former is tolerated as a necessary evil. The 'rationalist' has, being a disciplinarian, a horror of crude politics, be it 'teacher' or 'student' politicking through unions. These disturb the life of the mind; and interrupt, in unseemly ways, *coitus cognitus*. The ideal of a university is a citadel of knowledge without the *lumpens*, the loud-mouthed, politicking semi-literate students and teachers who mistake profoundly the area of knowledge with that of power.

Student and teacher 'politics' has to be tolerated as stoically as vice-chancellors who come and go, ruining in their movement *the* university as a site of reflective contemplation of matters which outlast daily acts of politicking. If the *lumpen* teachers bring about accelerated wage benefits, the prince among professors accepts these gracefully; these entitlements are an aspect of her natural right for which she could have waited in the certain knowledge that they cannot be thwarted for too long.

The 'hedonist' cannot, in contrast, avoid being immersed in campus politics; for her, everything becomes a matter of 'principles' despite the fact that nothing remains a matter of 'honour' in its rough and tumble. The 'hedonist' thinks she learns from real life struggle as much as through studies, teaching and research ; and has passionate commitment to altering the conditions and institutions in which knowledge is 'produced.' The 'hedonist' does not take conditions and processes of democracy as given but as ones created through acts of struggle. For her, knowledge and power are related, even to a point where one might have to say with Foucault that it is power which creates knowledge.

For the prince among scholars, teachers (who, as it were, consider teaching almost as a sensuous activity) constitute the *lumpen* elements, not to be allowed to storm the citadel of the aristocracy of the mind. For the best among the 'hedonistic' teachers, there is nothing but hostile pity for the best and the brightest rationalist who teach and know but have not lived; for, they have not experienced through teaching "the daring of a moment's surrender—which age of prudence cannot retrieve."

One could further refine and define these contrasts. You might say that they are overdrawn. Perhaps, but these point to differences not in degrees but rather of the kind. The difference is that between discipline and joy—a difference that comes dilemmatically alive in other arenas of life as well. And a difference which cannot be banished by awkward mutations such as "joyous discipline" or "disciplined joy."

IV

As a student in Rajkot, Bombay and Berkeley, and a teacher in Delhi and Duke, Sydney and Surat, I have lived with teachers and students who have proved living embodiments of some of these contrasts; and I have myself ambivalently moved from one to the other in time, place and circumstance.

In as impoverishing a society as India, and as turbulent and traumatically changeful, I do not feel quite at home with the rationalist model. And I have found that the understanding of the hedonistic approach, and acceptance of some of its elements, as catalytic not just for me as a teacher but for entire campuses, and more crucially the processes of life which surround campuses. For me, being a teacher in India is to be a deeply fractured, deeply wounded being, constantly in throes of transition, forever being evicted from utopias and yet, forbidden by history from desisting from struggles here and now for whatever 'justice' against injustice.

14
Sincerity in Teaching

SURESH C. GOEL

MINE is not a typical case: consider the fact that I started teaching M. Sc. classes at the tender age of 18 plus, the age at which Delhi University refuses to admit students to its postgraduate classes. I know that during these years I have changed a lot in my style of teaching as also in my ideas. Yet there is a continuity of basic principles, imposed by my personality.

Sometimes, around the time I was studying in high school, I had decided to go either into medicine or into teaching. As I grew older, I realised that I would not be able to enter the medical college till I had done my M. Sc. (previous); that was because of my young age. I, therefore, decided to join the teaching profession. Since I enjoy teaching, I have continued in the profession although there have been opportunities to take up other jobs.

After being appointed as a teacher I was asked to take up B.Sc. and M. Sc. classes. My very first lecture was to an M. Sc. class. Six out of eight students were my former class-fellows. Though a teacher, I was younger than they were. It weighed heavily on my mind as to what sort of relationship I should have with my former classmates now when they were my students. In fact, some of those in the B. Sc. class were also my former classmates. In this situation I had no choice except to decide on a few things. On the basis of my past experience these included erudition in the subject, uprightness in conduct, and fairness in dealing.

II

Although I had been a good student and had studied regularly throughout my undergraduate and postgraduate career, yet when I joined the teaching profession I found myself studying much more than what I had ever done as a student. When I was a student, I would hardly ever keep myself awake beyond midnight. After joining the teaching profession it was usual for me to keep awake till 1 o'clock or even 2 o'clock in the night. All this was necessary to read a number of books and to prepare notes. There has been a continuous desire, almost a compulsion, to impress the students, including those at the postgraduate level, that I had a mastery over the subject, that I had gone through almost all the books available in the library, that I had a clear grasp of the concepts and that I could be relied upon to give them the right information.

When I started, the method of teaching followed in that particular college was one which later in my career I found prudent to abandon. At the postgraduate level teachers used to go to the classroom with their well written notes and teach from the same. At the undergraduate level, on the other hand, the method of teaching followed was to deliver extempore lectures. In these classes, if one wanted to succeed as a teacher it was necessary that one should not refer to any notes or papers or books in the class. A teacher was supposed to know the subject and hold the attention of the students. Therefore, one had to be extra careful with undergraduate students.

Moreover, the undergraduate students always had a tendency to play pranks. The very first lecture with the B. Sc. class began with one. After reaching the classroom, I took the attendance of all the students despite the persistent demand that we should be first introduced to one another, according to the tradition of the college. I told them that we would do so once the attendance was over. So after the attendance, I gave them my name and a few other details and requested them to give me their names in turn. One of the prank-loving boys gave his name as Suresh Goel, the same as mine.

The class was obviously amused and waited to see my reactions. I asked the boy whether he was sure about his name and he replied "Yes, Sir". I immediately asked him either to leave the class or to produce a certificate from the Principal of he being a student of the class since, according to the attendance register, no boy with that name was supposed to be a member of the class. This put him in a tight corner; he was soon in a very apologetic mood. In this way I won the admiration of the other students who went on to introduce themselves in the proper way. This incident along with my work in preparing

Sincerity in Teaching

lectures and the helping attitude that I adopted towards the students helped me in gaining the confidence of the entire class by the end of the year.

With the passage of time I realised that there was one more factor in the teacher-student relationship. This is out-of-the-classroom behaviour of the teacher with the students. A teacher, I soon realised, has to behave as if, irrespective of his actual age, he is around 30-35 years. In addition to their search for knowledge, the students look to him for some mature advice in their personal affairs.

III

Apart from the academic scholarship, the most important single factor which I believe impresses the students most profoundly is the sense of fairness in dealings; a sense that a teacher treats all students equally, that he does not show favour to any student for reasons of caste, sex, relationship to influential people, or any other consideration. I have always been looked upon as a disciplinarian and, yet, I have always been highly respected. A couple of incidents in my experience confirmed this perception of mine.

In the very beginning I told every class that I would be the last person to enter the classroom and no student should enter the classroom once I was in. This was done to inculcate discipline among the students and also to develop in them a sense of responsibility towards the knowledge that they were going to get from the teacher. It has been my belief that students who come late to the class by a few minutes do not attach sufficient importance to the lectures that are delivered by the teacher. By the same token, students who reach in time for the examinations do so because they attach sufficient importance to examinations.

On the other hand, some students take it easy and conduct themselves in such a way that they reach the class just in time. If it so happens that they get delayed on the way for some reason, they become late for the class as well. My argument on the contrary always has been that they should try to reach the class full ten minutes ahead of the schedule. Anyway, since I made this a rule, I saw to it that everyone, irrespective of who he or she was, who was late, was politely told not to attend the lecture of the day. The students never complained about this matter although they often complained to me about other teachers regarding the same thing. Because of this self-imposed discipline, I could never afford to be late for the class even by two or three minutes.

The second instance concerns the attendance of the students. It had been the usual practice that if any student fell short of 75% attendance (the minimum requirement by the college to allow him to appear for the examination) towards the end of the year he would go to a particular teacher and request him to change the attendance rolls to enable him to appear in the examination. Since I had already told everyone in the beginning that I would not change the attendance in my register no student ever approached me with this request and there was never any friction between me and my students.

Fair dealing with students is a very important point, particularly in the case of biology teachers. This is because many teachers show a lenient attitude towards girl students. Being young, perhaps, some have a soft corner for them. Students, whether boys or girls, should be equally and fairly treated. And if you do not have a guilty conscience there is no reason to shy away from an open discussion on the matter.

Even before I joined the profession, because of my experience during the student days, I had made a very firm decision that one should have no romantic inclinations towards any student. This I did because of a particular incident. During our M. Sc. a few girls and boys went on excursion under the charge of a young teacher. This teacher unfortunately had some romantic inclination towards one of the girl students. Without giving many details it will suffice to state that due to this weakness of his he was much humiliated and I felt sorry for him.

In the very beginning of my career I found it advantageous to remain aloof in these matters. In a laboratory session I was watching the progress of the students from one end to the other with the experiment. When I had covered about 4 to 5 students and was explaining something to one of the girl students, a boy approached me and said that he wanted my urgent attention. A look at him and I could sense the non-serious nature of the request. So I very calmly told him to be seated and I would reach him once I was free after explaining what I was explaining. I also explained that I was following a sequence, starting from one end of the class to the other.

The boy replied that next time he would be sitting in the front seat of the class so that he could get attention earlier. At this I told him publicly that I would begin from any end of the class and, perhaps, from the end where this girl would be seated. He was nonplussed and realised that the game was up, and he could not push me into a corner. All this was possible, I believe, because I was clear in my mind about my motives and was even-handed with all my students.

Without mincing words and after a very long experience with a variety of students and a variety of college and university departments in U.P., Rajasthan and Maharashtra, I can say with confidence that if one is really fair, one may be as strict with the students as one likes; nobody ultimately objects to it. In the beginning some students may bear a grudge against the disciplinarian attitude of a teacher. They feel that one was only putting on a show of fairness without really being fair but in the long run, once they realise that one is not partial to any one, they accept all the discipline that one wishes to impose.

IV

The question of uprightness is very important for any teacher. A teacher not only imparts knowledge which a bright student in any case can get directly from books, he also presents a model before the students. When you are giving a lecture to a class of 60 students, obviously 120 eyes are watching you. These different persons who watch you have different backgrounds and watch different things in you. They watch not only your scholarship but also your manners, your dress and other things. When you give a lecture you not only talk about the subject, you also talk about many other things. These might include your comments on current affairs, on different personalities, on the social set up, on moral issues and so on.

Furthermore, students come to a teacher after the classroom to seek guidance, normally on the subject matter in hand but often on non-academic matters also. I, for one, have often been requested to give guidance and help sometimes even beyond my own experience of life. I can say with all honesty that I always attempted to guide the students to the best of my ability even in matters non-academic. In fact, many a time a student has no one else to go to for guidance except a teacher in whom he has confidence.

A student can confide in such a teacher and the student believes that because of his scholarship as well as his comparative maturity the teacher can put him on the right path. As time passes, these models of behaviour seem to be getting a low priority. Most teachers nowadays, I am afraid, do not feel called upon to present such a model before the students. They argue, with which I disagree, that present day students do not look upon a teacher with reverence and that a student selects his model of behaviour mainly from persons other than his teachers.

To me the relationship between a teacher and students is very important. I do not think that a student can really learn from you unless you command his respect, and if you wish to have his respect you have to be worthy of it. A teacher has little option in this regard. One of the important preconditions for commanding the respect of students is upright behaviour. An instance of how reasonable and rational students can be should be found in order.

I was to engage an undergraduate class. When I reached the class, the students told me that they wished to go on a strike for which a call had been given by the Students Union. I found out that the strike call had been given because, due to their connections with certain ministers, some students had been admitted to the medical college in an irregular way. Thereupon I said that if that was true I did not see any reason why I should not lead the *morcha* to the Vice-Chancellor; but only on one condition.

This delighted the students but they got a little suspicious also; they waited to hear my condition. I told them that I too was prepared to lead the *morcha* if all of them took the oath that none of them would use their influence or connections for gaining an undue advantage in life. I added that if something came their way without any effort, they may accept it. All I wanted them was to pledge that they would not strive for an undue advantage for themselves.

These remarks dramatised my position which was that if they were not sure that they could live with such high standards of conduct, they had no justification to go on a strike. I did not accept the position that if anyone of them had a minister to help them, they would do the same which the others had done. I told them that I did not approve of what had been done but neither did I approve of a strike on this issue at the cost of their study unless they could make a beginning towards self reform.

V

In India there is no training programme to learn teaching methods, at least as far as teachers in colleges and universities are concerned. So a prospective teacher has to be on the job without any preparation, and the only models that he has before him are those of the teachers who taught him. After having taught for quite some years I am fully convinced that the same teaching methods are not suitable for students studying in different classes such as secondary students, undergraduates, and postgraduates, nor are the same methods equally suitable for students of the sciences and the humanities. The very requirements of teaching are different for undergraduates as compared to postgraduates. At the postgraduate level it is most essential that students get training in self-learning and not simply in receiving and memorising the facts, or even simple analysis of the facts given to them by a teacher. This means that a postgraduate teacher must make a special effort to inculcate in the students the habit of learning as also the presentation of the material by the students after a careful analysis of information from various sources.

One of the methods which I found suitable for this purpose was to assign each student a particular topic and ask him to present it before the class. Every member of the class should also be requested to read the topic beforehand and encouraged to stop the student if there is some error of facts or of their interpretation. This method I found not only encourages self-learning but also develops a spirit of enquiry and questioning.

I have found that students are quite enthusiastic about asking questions from fellow students but not so much from the teacher. The role of a teacher during such seminars is to oversee that no wrong information is being given by the student and no major aspect of the subject in question has been omitted. This method has the added advantage of active participation of students in teaching. This may not be the method to be used for secondary school students but it certainly can be tried out with the undergraduate students.

A postgraduate teacher should lead students to acquire more and more knowledge but not stultify their thinking. Therefore, even the lectures given by the postgraduate teacher should have an openness in their approach to the subject. Unfortunately, many teachers in the country, including those in the universities, still consider a monologue called a lecture to be the best method of teaching by a teacher. Some of them actually still dictate notes which probably they had prepared quite some time back.

VI

One of the most important aspects of the training of science students is laboratory work. Right from the British days, marks assigned to practical work at the B.Sc. and M.Sc. level are between one third and one half of the total marks. Moreover, the time spent on practicals in the laboratory is usually as much as that spent on lectures in the classroom. Even so, it is only a rare science teacher who realises the importance of conducting practicals.

It must be emphasised here that the knowledge that any science teacher imparts to his students in theory lectures has passed through several hands: the original research worker, the review writer and the author of the book. The knowledge that the students get in the practicals is first hand. In the practical a teacher and a student are on the same plane of obtaining knowledge. A student must observe all that a teacher can; a teacher cannot resort to his authority to demonstrate something which is missing in the practicals.

In the practicals, the student learns the art of keen, unbiassed observation which is so difficult to acquire. At the same time the student learns how the messy bench data is later converted into clean paper data. It is with the help of practicals that a student acquires the art of the right interpretation of results. In short, the student comes face to face with scientific methodology only during his laboratory sessions.

Confirmation of the already recorded observations, and interpretations by the student in the laboratory gives him the confidence to believe in the rest of the knowledge that he acquires from the book and which he has neither the time nor the facilities to verify. It is important, therefore, that laboratory experiments are conducted even more seriously than the classroom lectures. Unfortunately, this rarely happens. Many teachers delegate the work of supervising laboratory sessions to their research scholars, and many senior teachers do not wish to supervise the laboratory work. It is my opinion that senior teachers should invariably associate themselves with the supervision of laboratory work. I have seen students in M.Sc. Life Science classes who while observing a cell in a section under the microscope confuse the nucleus with a cell and the nucleolus with a nucleus. This is after they have ostensibly been observing the cells during the preceding five years.

Our indifference to practicals is reflected in the quality of research that our students do later on. They have never learnt the art of keen, unbiassed observation or interpretation of results or writing. I am, therefore, of the definite view that teachers should spend much time and effort in laboratory sessions with the students, and at the same time ensure that students do not complete the record at home, from books and other sources.

VII

The interaction between a Ph.D. student and his guide, particularly in the science subjects, is of a very special nature. The student and the guide have to adjust to each other not only in their working habits but also in their thinking and outlook. Most often, by the time a Ph.D. student submits his thesis, he is quite fed up with the guide and most students wish that they had no future relationship with him. The guide, on the other hand, feels relieved. The relationship between the two can be pleasing also if the guide has the requisite human qualities.

A Ph.D. student comes to have a very close look at the personality of his guide and comes to appreciate not only his scholarship but also the ego problems involved and the adjustments necessary. To be a guide of a Ph.D. student, a teacher must have a high intellectual calibre and integrity. In fact, in the present educational system the only place where the old *guru-shishya* relationship really comes into play is in the relationship between a guide and his Ph.D. student.

Difficulties usually start arising at the time of making observations when experiments are conducted. The art of unbiassed observations is extremely difficult. It gives a shock to a confident student to become aware of the carelessness with which he has been observing things during his pre-Ph.D. days. The second point of conflict usually arises at the time of the interpretation of results. But the most crucial conflict is normally at the end; at the time of writing the thesis. It is at this stage that a whole lot of difficulties surface.

It is only during the Ph.D. training that a teacher has to demonstrate to the students the art of thinking, the art of observation, the art of writing, the art of interpretation and the art of drawing conclusions. Of course this is so only when a guide knows himself how to do research and desires that his students are properly trained in research methodology and hopes that the publication from his laboratory will add to scientific knowledge. No scientist or teacher, however highly placed or busy he may be, has the right to delegate the responsibility of teaching a Ph.D. student to a junior colleague or a senior student.

I consider myself lucky in the fact that all my Ph.D. students have had most cordial relations with me. This is perhaps due to their ability to adjust to all the demands that I make upon them. In course of time they come to see that these demands were for their good and not due to any illwill towards them. It is said that the relationship between a Ph. D. student and his guide should not be exploited for non-academic reasons. This relationship tests the personality of the guide to his maximum. In our country, I make bold to say, there are guides who exploit students. To me this is academic corruption of the worst order. We may have a research assistant, research associates and technicians to help us do our research and explore our ideas in the laboratory. The research scholars fall in a different category and should be treated as such.

VIII

One of the important lacuna in the teaching system is the absence of the job description of a teacher. This is applicable both to universities and colleges. What are the responsibilities of a teacher is a question that has been asked by many but a proper answer has been hard to get. In the present context, the University Grants Commission has suggested three equally important activities for a teacher. These are teaching, research and extension work.

I do not think that his completes the list of activities of a teacher. For example, to organise students in healthy groups for sports, cultural activities and similar other joyful occupations is also important. Many teachers are long remembered by their students not because of what they taught or even how they taught but what advice did the teacher gave to the student in times of difficulty or how helpful the teacher has been to them in various non-academic matters. It is, therefore, difficult to define qualities of a good teacher in an absolute manner. Though a good teacher is said to be one who is: "An interesting man or woman, a determined person with a sense of humour, good memory and kindness. He must know his subject and like it and like his pupils" (G. Highet, 1952, *The Art of Teaching*).

IX

Recently I joined Indira Gandhi National Open University (IGNOU), which is a new and challenging experiment in the field of higher education in India. The role of a teacher in distance education is quite different from that of a teacher in a conventional university. In this system it is "teachers at the headquarters" who are primarily responsible for imparting education; they never meet the students studying around the country in their respective homes. The only knowledge a student has about a teacher is through his writings or explanations on video-tapes.

One of the important features of distance education is the network of the student support system. Under this system, many study centres thoughout the country will cater to the needs of the students. Each study centre will have a library of books, audio and video materials and will appoint academic counsellers for the guidance of students. Each student will have an individual counseller to whom he may go in order to get his difficulties removed. Even so, the student may have no one to turn to so as to seek explanation of a difficult piece of writing while reading at home. Consequently teachers have to foresee the difficulties that students might face.

In this system a student will often lack the classroom atmosphere of the peer group. The preparation of the printed self-study material, therefore, is a specialized task. It has to keep up the motivation of the student, must be easy to understand, self-contained and of high academic standard. Unlike the conventional universities where a teacher may get away after imparting insufficient or wrong information in his lectures, a teacher in an open university has to be very careful, in fact punctilious. The material prepared by him becomes available for review and criticism by the best scholars in the country.

The printed study material of IGNOU, in my opinion, is likely to have far reaching academic consequences. It may bring about a minor revolution at the undergraduate level in the country. Presently, in several conventional universities, the quality of information imparted to students is indifferent and the quantity is meagre. It is difficult to place responsibility for this state of affairs; policy-makers, teachers, students, politicians and the social milieu, all have contributed to it.

The monitoring of the quality of education is traditionally missing in universities and colleges. In many universities the number of teaching days gets severely curtailed, and, yet, no one cares. Some teachers do not teach to the best of their ability. The method of examination in universities promotes the mushroom growth of guide books. The UGC scheme of producing quality textbooks through its 'Book-Writing Scheme' has also not produced the desired results. Consequently, even committed teachers do not find it easy to update the syllabi or do the job to their entire satisfaction. Good students desirous of acquiring knowledge are also not able to exert any influence in the matter. One of the important reasons for this is the non-availability of printed material of a high academic level in simple language and at a reasonable price.

The printed study material of IGNOU will overcome this difficulty. It will not be possible to prepare examination-oriented "guide books" in respect of this study material. The material is produced by a team of subject experts from all over the country, under the supervision of distance education experts and IGNOU faculty. The easy availability of this material is likely to embolden the committed teacher and students to exert pressure on the university system to update the syllabi and bring about other changes. This in turn casts a special responsibility on the IGNOU to keep updating the syllabi and also keep abreast of educational technology.

A teacher of IGNOU gets academic feedback from students through the academic counsellors. All the same a teacher loses the refreshing touch with his students. But it is a matter of satisfaction for all teachers in the Open University that they will be contributing towards the democratization of education. We hope that knowledge reaches everyone, wheresoever located and whatever the age or status, without the person having to give up his job.

The most difficult part of distance education is the planning and

Sincerity in Teaching

conduct of the laboratory exercises in the science subject. Laboratory training is a vital component of science education. In the open university system, this task requires considerable innovation and a departure from the routine.

To identify the objectives of various practical exercises and to evolve suitable methods to fulfill the same requires careful consideration. Due to the limitation imposed by the distance mode of education the practical sessions may eventually be fewer in number but the exercises will be precisely designed to develop manual and observational skills, and skills to formulate a problem, develop a hypothesis, design an experiment to test the hypothesis, and to interpret the results. Sometimes it may become necessary to train those teachers who will conduct practicals. Normally video programmes will be prepared to help teachers and students to perform the practicals in a proper manner.

The conduct of practicals will be according to a flexible schedule. In this regard, three systems are under consideration. The students may perform laboratory exercises in the evenings or on weekends at study centres in the well equipped laboratories of colleges. Alternatively, they may choose to undergo intensive training for a period of about three weeks every year in laboratories especially set up by IGNOU for this purpose.

A redeeming feature of the experiment called the open university system of education is that the best scholars in the country are involved in this task and in guiding IGNOU towards its goal: Education for all.

X

Based on my limited experience of teaching, these have been some of the random thoughts that have occurred to me. If we wish teachers to have a place of honour in the community of professionals, the teachers have to continuously upgrade their professional skills and have a code of conduct for the discharge of their professional duties. They must have a commitment to their subject, to their students and to the nation. Teachers are often criticised for doing very little work and for having too many holidays. There is no doubt that some teachers do give room for such comments to be made about them.

In my opinion, a teacher should remain a student throughout his life. Those who do not aspire for scholarship should give up the teaching profession. The policy-makers must put their heads together and see, in pragmatic terms, what sort of incentives and facilities need to be given to teachers. At one time, a few universities encouraged teachers to purchase books, by sharing 50 per cent of the cost of the purchase of books. Such practices have unfortunately been discontinued. Similarly, the practice of holding summer institutes has been discontinued because of its abuse by certain individuals. The facilities to do research in the university are so meagre that the less said about them, the better.

It might be interesting to find out how much a university-appointed teacher in a university will get on average as research fund if all the research fund available in the country were taken into consideration and divided equally among the teachers. This is just to indicate the anomaly between research funding on the one hand and the requirement from the teachers that they should do some quality research on the other hand.

15

On Being a Teacher

AMRIK SINGH

WITHIN a few days of my having completed my Master's examination I got a teaching post in a college. Overnight, from a student I became a teacher. Nobody told me how to go about my new job. Since I had been a student for sixteen years, it was open to me to refer to the models that I had observed for myself as a student. And that is exactly what I proceeded to do.

I recalled very little of my early teachers. One of them who taught me in my fifth standard stood out as a picturesque character but what I remembered of him was two of us sitting on one bench in the class. My fellow student was in the habit of bringing ample quantities of peanuts to the class and eating the nuts while teaching was in progress. Since he sat next to me and would press them on me, I also got into the habit. This was not liked by this particular teacher. Whenever he caught us munching nuts in the class, and that was quite often, he would walk up to us (in order to escape his direct gaze we usually occupied a bench in the second row) and give each of us a couple of blows. Sometimes he even twisted our arms. It used to hurt but it did not discourage us from going ahead with what we were doing. As soon as we found that he was not observing us, we would get back to our routine. The punishment given to us never stopped us from doing what we were doing. When I grew older and looked back on the series of incidents, I found that most children at that age do exactly this kind of thing; it is all a part of growing up.

There were one or two other incidents like that which stand out in my memory. But as far as the impact of any teachers on me was concerned, I did not recall anything clearly or distinctly. When I was an undergraduate, however, there were two teachers of mine who made a profound impression on my mind. One of them was slow, methodical and lucid. When he finished teaching, one could almost reproduce word for word what he had taught. As far as the art of communication was concerned, he was unrivalled in his skill as well as effectiveness. But there was another equally effective teacher and he also produced a deep impression on my mind. He was not very methodical but he would explore the topic in hand in considerable depth. He would help us to see a particular topic from various points of view. He would not draw any definite conclusion which could be reproduced in so many words. What he succeeded in doing was to leave us with a feeling that there was much more to learn than he had the time to communicate. This in turn quite often persuaded us to go to the library and explore the topic in further detail.

When I started teaching, these two models were there in front of me. I had to make a choice. I could adopt one or the other. Within a few weeks, however, I discovered that this was not the right way of posing the question. It is not always open to a teacher to choose a particular model. So much depends upon his own interest and pre-disposition.

To cut the story short, it took me a few months to discover that while I did have some ability for orderly presentation, I perhaps lacked the gift for lucidity, which one of my models had possessed. At the same time, I felt greatly interested in the other teacher's capacity to arouse curiosity and enthusiasm and prompt us to learn for ourselves. This state of mind invariably used to send me to the library and I usually explored further for myself whatever I had been told in the class. I felt that this aspect of teaching was an important aspect, perhaps the most valuable one.

As already stated, I discovered that what a newly recruited teacher takes from another model is not only what he likes to take but also what he can take. In other words, the individual's capacity to model himself is no less important than the effectiveness of the model. All this was not clear to me in the beginning. It became clear to me step by step and I am inclined to think that this is likely to be as true of others as it was of me.

II

Something significant in personal terms happened at the end of the fourth month after I had started teaching. I decided to quit my first job and move to another. According to my terms of appointment I had to give one week's notice. During this one week the response of both my colleagues and students was uncommonly warm and cordial. Several of my colleagues tried to dissuade me from leaving that particular institution. But what took me by total surprise was the fact that the day I was to leave, almost half the college strength turned up at the railway station. The college was within half a mile of the railway station and therefore there was no problem of transport. At the same time, it was an extraordinary sight; there were several hundred students milling about the railway platform.

Even before the train steamed off, I must confess I broke down. So much affection was being showered on me that when the train started moving, I was literally in tears and was pushed into the train by those standing around me. For the next hour or so I was in a state of deep melancholy. I was not very certain in my mind if I had done the right thing in leaving that bunch of students. During the next couple of years, I kept on receiving letters from several of them. Then came the partition of the country and everything got disrupted. Every now and then, however, I run into some of those students and it is heart-warming to interact with them once again.

There was also another reason why the experience of the first four months moved me so deeply. Before I opted to go into teaching, I had toyed with the idea of going into journalism. One of my teachers who happened to be around at that time almost decided the matter for me when he said to my father, "A bird in hand is worth two in the bush." I had already been offered a teaching position without my having had to apply for it and to reject it in favour of an uncertain future was more than my family was prepared to accept.

While I cannot say that I have outgrown my interest in journalism completely, it is clear to me that in opting for teaching I had taken the right decision. The memory of several hundred students turning up to bid me good-bye after I had been in contact with them only for four months had no meaning other than this. Never again in my career, except for some fleeting moments, did I have second thoughts with regard to the career that I had opted for.

One thing should be clear by now. Nobody had instructed me with regard to the art of teaching. I had to rely entirely on my own and the only worthwhile thing that I could do was to recall how some of my teachers for whom I had respect had gone about it. In plain words, it amounted to learning on the job. Looking back it is clear to me that had I been instructed in advance, I could have avoided some of the mistakes that I did make. This does not refer to the understanding of the subject. To some extent, before one starts teaching one has already come to grips with the subject as a student and one has also learnt the technique of learning more about it. In any case learning is a never-ending process and one keeps learning all the time. It is the technique of teaching that has to be learnt at that stage. I have no doubt in my mind that some kind of training imparted in this regard would be found useful.

Let us take the obvious question of what is the objective of teaching. Is it communication of information? Is it ability to understand interconnections? Is it the ability to apply what one has learnt to the problems and situations that one is confronted with? Is it to inspire the student to know more about the subject and to explore it in greater depth? Is it a combination of all these or is one element to be emphasised more than the others? There is a whole host of issues here. How is a new-comer to grapple with these issues and find answers to them? In other words, at the time of his initiation, were a teacher to be made aware of the range and possibilities of his profession, it would be immensely useful. Equally important, it would make him a more effective and efficient teacher.

There is also a related question. Everything is given in books, more particularly in a textbook addressed to a particular level of competence. Why should it be necessary for a teacher to explain all that is contained in the book? Why cannot a student do without the teacher and go to the textbook directly? Does the teacher have a role in addition to the book that is written out for him by another teacher or scholar?

All these are questions which presented themselves to me one by one. I cannot say which one arose first and which one came next. At this distance of time from where I started, I cannot recall the sequence in which these questions shaped themselves in my mind. All that I can say is that I had no clear and categorical answers to them. It is only over the years that to some extent I have been able to formulate a certain philosophy of teaching for myself. I cannot say whether it has the sanction of scholarship behind it. There is hardly any significant reading that I have done on the subject. Here and there I have stumbled upon a few things. Most often I have found that my ideas which I developed through by own experience of teaching had got confirmed, though I must add that in a few cases my ideas were greatly stimulated by the few hints that I came upon in those books and articles.

III

To answer the latter question first, it should be clear to everyone that no one can do without a teacher. One learns not only from a teacher in the classroom but keeps on learning from everyone one comes in contact with. Our parents are our earliest teachers. But we learn from our siblings and friends as well. What we learn in the classroom (it applies only to those in our country who do get into the formal system) is important and provides the foundation on which most subsequent learning is based. But apart from the intellectual foundation that is given to us by our teachers there are several other things that we learn and indeed have to learn. Informal learning is in this sense an important input.

Most of this was clear to me when I started teaching. But what was not clear to me at that stage was that the role of the teacher was important not only as a provider of knowledge but also as a model. There are those who cannot join the formal system and model themselves on whoever they happen to come in contact with. It may be a parent, it may be a cousin, it may be a neighbour or a friend. Whoever be the model, he has a crucial role to play. In the formal system however this role is quite often played by the teacher. He is older than the student and the latter therefore looks up to him. This was not particularly clear to me in the early years of my teaching. But two incidents within the first couple of years of my teaching career brought home this lesson to me powerfully.

In one case, I left station without permission and did so by cutting a somewhat inconvenient class in the afternoon of a Thursday. Friday and Saturday happened to be holidays and I therefore took a long weekend off. On Monday when I came back I was told that the Principal had been looking for me. I felt guilty, I thought that the Principal had come to know about my having played truant and I would therefore have to explain why I had chosen to act in this delinquent way. After a couple of hours when I happened to see the

Principal, he asked me about something else, and this thing was not referred to at all. Evidently he had not heard about my having cut a class.

However, those 2-3 hours of acute self-reproach that I had gone through had a remarkably chastening effect on me. I said to myself that never again would I do such a stupid thing. In the background was also a guilty feeling that by playing truant I had not set a good example to my students. It was more or less for the first time that the moral aspect of my conduct as a teacher appeared in a new light to me. This aspect of the problem had not presented itself to me earlier as sharply as it did on that occasion. The fact of the matter is that my having played truant stemmed from the fact that I had been somewhat casual in my approach to teaching. Without having been prepared for it, I was now required to face the moral implications of what I had done. I did not like the look of it and I promised to myself that in future whatever I do must be defensible, both morally and publicly.

Another incident which happened around that time reinforced this feeling. For the first couple of years when one starts teaching, there is not much of an age gap between the teacher and the student. One was a student only yesterday and today one is already a member of the teaching staff. It takes some time to get accustomed to the new role. It was in this undefined state of my role that something happened which made me aware of the fact that I was very much on the other side of the fence, that is, a teacher.

A student whom I knew rather well and who used to visit me frequently came to see me one winter evening. He had been summoned by the Principal in connection with an incident in which a friend of this student was involved. The Principal knew that this student was privy to all that had happened and he wanted him to reveal everything. Out of loyalty to his friend, this particular student refused to do so. The Principal told him thereupon that if he was not prepared to be forthcoming, the Principal would have no choice but to rusticate him.

Immediately after the meeting with the Principal, the student came to see me. He wanted me to advise him in the situation in which he found himself. It was a difficult situation, but more important than that was the question if it was right for me to advise him. From 6 p.m. to 1 a.m. we kept on talking. The student had his dinner with me and I

On Being a Teacher

eventually also offered him lodging for the night. Every few minutes he would ask me what he should do. My answer was that it was for him to decide and all that I could do was to discuss the issue with him. On several occasions he decided to reveal everything and on as many occasions he decided against it. In the end we both decided to go to sleep and discuss the matter the following morning.

Seven hours later the student said that he had made up his mind and he was not going to squeal on his friend. What his friend had done was certainly objectionable and he himself had not approved of it. Only he knew what his friend was going to do and all that could be said against him was that he had not dissuaded his friend. Nonetheless, he felt that he could not let him down and he told me that he had made up his mind to that effect. I thereupon advised him to send a telegram to his father. That was done and before the evening was out his father had arrived. I explained the whole situation to him. The father persuaded the Principal to let his son migrate to another college and this is how the issue was resolved. That the student eventually did not pursue his studies in the other college and decided to join the Indian Navy (it was war time) is another matter.

The point I am trying to make is that, unknown to myself and without being at all prepared for it, I was faced with a situation which unmistakably had moral dimensions. Looking back it is clear to me that I handled the situation as it should have been handled. But this much needs to be underlined that I had no training or preparation for what I had encountered. I had played by the ear, as they say. Fortunately, no serious mistake was made and both I and the student did what was the right thing to do. Had I faltered or had that young boy faltered, it would have been difficult to live with the consequences.

Situations like these can arise in the life of any teacher and indeed they do arise. More than anything else, it underlines the point that a teacher cannot always be a neutral or a passive character. A teacher has got to be somebody who knows his mind and can conduct himself in such a situation with a due sense of responsibility. What he does will have consequences if not for him, at least for the students, and this is a responsibility that cannot be trifled with.

IV

Two issues emerge from what has been said so far. What are the objectives that one should have in mind when one enters a classroom and faces a group of students who in theory are interested in being taught but in actual practice are not all that keen? The second issue relates to the kind of model that one has to project of oneself as a teacher. While in regard to the second issue it took me many more years to clarify my ideas, the first issue had to be resolved within the first year.

In our situation, the parameters of what one does in the classroom are set in advance. The syllabus is laid down and the books are prescribed. Theoretically speaking, it is open to a student to read the books on his own and instruct himself. In actual practice this does not happen. Students almost everywhere, and not only in our country, require to be introduced to the topic under discussion. Though they are curious, yet they give evidence of a certain kind of reluctance to accept the logic of their curiosity. Were they genuinely and seriously curious, they could seek the answers themselves. Everything is contained in the books available to them as well as to the teacher. But something has to happen before the students get turned on.

This something has to be done by the teacher. To what extent he succeeds in doing so depends upon his skill, his enthusiasm and his energy. The word energy should be understood in its widest sense. Physical energy is important but undue importance need not be attached to it. Very few teachers suffer from that lack of energy which would undermine their ability to instruct as well as interact with students. Most often what they are deficient in is enthusiasm and not energy. The two are related to each other to some extent but are not exactly the same.

It is intellectual energy which is more important and more relevant to the task in hand. A teacher having preceded the students in the quest for knowledge has already traversed the path that he wants his students to take. He is familiar with all the turns and twists and curves and bends. He had done his own part of the slogging necessary for the purpose. What he has to do now is to arouse the curiosity and enthusiasm of his students to that when he goes over the familiar and well traversed path, others can follow him.

Equally important, he also knows the pace that he must set for himself in the classroom. An experienced teacher will know when to go slow and when to quicken his pace. So much depends upon the response that he is getting from his students. His experience will tell him that while some can keep pace with him, others cannot. He has therefore to repeat himself, and sometimes more than once. There would still be a few of them left who perhaps cannot keep up even with the slower pace. Unless their number is large, and usually it is not, they can be ignored, though sometimes to do so can prove costly and one has to go over the whole thing once again. All these are matters which come with experience; later on he learns much more quickly than he would otherwise.

Still the question would arise: what is the objective that one sets before one's self? Is it simply to impart information or something more than that? A minimal amount of information has to be imparted, otherwise one is just not understood. How detailed or skimpy it should be depends upon the group of students one is handling, their level of alertness or otherwise, the particular topic that one is having to deal with and a number of other equally pertinent considerations. Some information has to be imparted without question. Unless this is done, the process of teaching lacks body and fails to make an impact.

But mere information is not enough. It has also got to be related to what a student already knows. In other words, information is not something abstract or lifeless. Information is a living tissue and, even if it is not, it must be made a living thing so that what is being stated on that day and what was stated on an earlier occasion can be integrated by the student in terms of his own understanding and his capability. This process ultimately leads to a qualitative change in the mind of the student whereby information becomes knowledge. There are a number of intermediate steps also.

The imparting of information is only a step towards the acquisition of knowledge. It is a necessary step, indeed an indispensable step, but to stop merely at the giving of information and not integrate it with what the student already knows is to do grave disservice to him. Instead of getting illumined with new insights he gets confused. Quite some teachers achieve this somewhat unintended result. Clearly they do not know the art of teaching. The art of teaching lies in being able to integrate what is being taught with what the student already knows. This is what makes it possible for a student to acquire new insights. Unless this can be ensured, there is something wrong somewhere.

Once information has graduated into knowledge, issues like establishing interconnections, applying what one has learnt to the problems and situations that one encounters, cease to be issues. With a high degree of understanding thus achieved, there would be a natural desire in the mind of student to know much more than what a teacher has been able to give him. This is what would send him to the library or to the laboratory. In addition to everything else, a teacher must arouse this desire to know more in the minds of the students. Being able to inspire one's students is the highest peak of success that a teacher can reach. That only a few of them can do so only indicates how difficult it is to reach this level of excellence. Whether this objective is reached or not, there cannot be any exception to the well-recognised truth that ultimately all education is self-education.

In practical terms, therefore, a teacher's first job is to introduce the topic that he has to handle. The process of learning, however, does not stop here. This is only the beginning. When a student has been introduced to something, he goes back to his textbook and what is stated there now begins to make sense to him. He could have gone to the textbook in the first instance too. Only he was lazy or, more likely, somewhat unenterprising. The teacher having aroused his interest sends him to the textbook.

If this interest has been aroused, he will not stop at the textbook. He would also like to go to those books on the basis of which the textbook is written. This does not happen in every case. This describes an ideal situation. To what extent it happens in one case and not in another would simply indicate the kind of student that an individual is. He can be a good student, he can be an indifferent one and, equally probable, he can be a bad student. A teacher would, however, do well not to admit to himself that any student is a bad student. The acceptable thing should be that some are slow learners and others are late learners; but a learner everyone is and is expected to be.

The role of the teacher is therefore crucial. He is the one that shows the way. He is the one who kindles the students' curiosity and interest. He is the one that encourages them to follow the path shown by him. In a few cases the students get so wrapped up in what the teacher has told them that they travel very fast and sometimes even go ahead of the teacher. This does not happen at the early stages. But it does sometimes happen at the terminal stages. As and when it happens, it is a cause for celebration. The success of a teacher lies in producing students who outstrip him. This is how scholarship grows and this is how progress take place.

V

In respect of the second issue—the teacher as a model—one thing requires to be clearly understood. Some people like other human beings; others do not feel at ease with them and in that situation manage to do whatever they are capable of. In my opinion, the second category of persons should not go into teaching. One prerequisite for teaching is that one must like other human beings. This alone makes human interaction possible, even a source of pleasure. Competence or interest in a particular discipline, for instance, is a good preparation for a research career. But it is not necessarily a good preparation for a teaching career. In order to be a teacher, the ability to get on with people is crucial. Even more crucial is the desire to help others to grow and prosper. Those who look upon others as their 'enemy' may think of any other career but not teaching.

Interaction with students is a part of the job that one enters upon. There is interaction within the class as well as outside the class. Within the class, for instance, situations arise and those have to be dealt with on the spot. Most of those situations are different expressions of inter-personal tensions and conflicts. Those who know how to get on with others without friction and how to 'manage' other people succeed better than those who are seldom at ease in the company of others. This is not the occasion to go into the various irritations that can and do arise and the ways to overcome them. That is a separate issue by itself and requires independent discussion. But there is no doubt that the ability to like other human beings and the desire to see them grow into men and women of whom one can be proud, are basic to the teaching situation.

In my experience I have come across quite a number of colleagues who were misfits in the profession. This is not being said with reference to their capability. Some of them were capable without question. But they lacked the ability to get on with other people and were not interested in others as human beings. To some extent, one has to have the same sense of involvement and pride as a teacher as parents have in respect of their children. It is a joy to be able to bring up children. It should be equally a joy to instruct one's students, to see them grow in knowledge and understanding and shape into human beings with the right values and the right attitudes. Somebody once defined education as dissemination of certain attitudes through appropriate skills. While not a complete definition, it says a good deal in regard to what education is about.

There is yet another dimension of teaching which it would be a folly to ignore or underplay. The most important influences in the life of any one are those of the mother and the teacher. The mother's influence stays as long as one lives. In the case of the teacher the influence is much more diffused and somewhat patchy. As a student one is taught by several teachers. While quite a few of them can be influential, it is usually one teacher at a time whose influence dominates and it is that particular influence which to a large extent shapes a student's destiny. Or is it putting it too strongly?

When the stakes are so high, the question to ask is: Can a teacher afford not to take his responsibility? A word of praise or blame means so much to the student. Both acceptance and rejection have a world of meaning for him. Therefore, no student can be indifferent to what his teacher thinks of him. A careless word or a false move by the teacher can have long-range implications. Whether he likes it or not, a teacher without being fully aware of what he is entering upon, has chosen a career where every step taken by him is appraised and every move of his is watched.

In any other profession he can be a private citizen. A teacher, even if he wishes to divest himself of the role thrust upon him, cannot help the fact that what he does or fails to do will influence the students who come into contact with him. Clearly it is a difficult role to play and not everyone succeeds in playing the role as well as he should.

VI

While one had to learn the craft of teaching within a year or so, the other dimension of teaching took much longer to understand and live upto. Two of the incidents that made me aware of this particular dimension have been referred to already. It should not be necessary to refer to several others which brought home the same points to me. All that I can say is that when I recall some of them, I still feel red in the face. Amongst the lapses of which I was guilty, lack of candour was perhaps the most forgivable. But there were several others which showed me in an unfavourable light. I had no choice, however, except to live with them and to some extent learn from them.

In this connection, one thing has to be borne in mind. Young people, if they are not handled properly, do not easily forgive. Their contact with the teachers may be transitory in character but what is done to them stays with them much longer. On numerous occasions I have come across students who will refer to some of their experiences as students, not with nostalgia but with bitterness. Only those who were the cause of this bitterness are not around to hear what the students had to say.

Normally speaking, the dominant feeling in the minds of students should be one of gratitude. When they recall their teachers in later life they should remember them with gratitude for whatever they had learnt and not live with bitterness as several of them do. Bitterness, even when it exists, should melt away with years. But if it stays with some people, it may be a comment upon the kind of human beings that they are. At the same time, it is an indication of the damage done to them.

Two things that most students do not forgive are lack of fairness and any kind of pretence on the part of the teachers. It is an unequal situation in which students find themselves; teachers are at the giving end and students are at the receiving end. Though at a disadvantage, they expect the teachers to hold the scales even and to be fair in their dealings. This does not always happen. Sometimes students protest and sometimes they cannot do so for reasons of propriety, discretion and several other reasons. In some rare cases they are vocal in their protest but that is usually on a collective basis and seldom as individuals. Lack of fairness betokens, amongst other things, lack of respect for them. They resent it and the surest way of alienating them is not to give them what is due to them.

The second deadly sin is pretence. If a teacher pretends to be what he is not, sooner or later students find it out. A teacher may pretend to be learned whereas he may not even have prepared that day's lecture. He may pretend to be a hundred other things. But whatever be the pretence, it wears thin in the eyes of students. One can pretend with people whom one meets occasionally. But to pretend in front of people who observe one at very close quarters is to invite ridicule. Not only that, students closely watch to what extent a teacher is consistent in respect of what he says and what he does. Any kind of deviation between the two is immediately noticed. The student response, whether expressed or unexpressed, is always critical in such a situation. In the long run no one can win the esteem and respect of his students unless he comes across as a person whose profession and practice were not inconsistent with each other.

Step by step as the meaning of it all unfolded itself to me, I felt trapped: I had opted for a profession where mistakes, if made, were likely to look much bigger than they would have been otherwise. It was an awful burden to carry. Having once entered the profession there was no going back. This is not to imply that teachers have to be infallible and operate on the plane of moral rectitude all the time. To say such a thing would be to stretch the point. But this much has to be accepted that in the profession of teaching the search for perfection is unrelenting. From this point of view, whether it is an ideal profession to adopt or not can be a matter for opinion. Speaking for myself, I have no regrets, though I must confess in all honesty that on occasions I have found the burden much heavier than my frail shoulders could carry.

While every professional is self-conscious about what he sets out to do, a teacher has of necessity to be much more self-conscious. He is dealing with human beings and not with products and processes. Human beings are fallible, subject to moods and whims and prone to all kinds of unexpected, even irrational, decisions. To deal with them, therefore, requires an extraordinary degree of sensitivity which in psychological terms is described as empathy. To be able to respond to other human beings as human beings is almost a prerequisite for being a successful teacher.

VII

Apart from the feeling of empathy that has got to be a part of one's mental and emotional make-up, in order to be a successful teacher there has to be a firm and clear-sighted recognition of the objectives that one has in view. Objectives are important because one cannot teach otherwise, nor can one design the syllabus or evolve a strategy of teaching. Even assessment of students is not possible unless there is broad agreement on what one sets out to do and what one succeeds in doing. The primary objectives therefore must be recognised. It goes without saying that the objectives must be clearly defined. Only they should not be rigid or inflexible. It should always be possible to adjust to the changing situation.

In this connection, it is important to make distinctions in respect of the various stages of education. For instance, children at the nursery and primary levels are highly malleable. What teachers require most often at that stage is the ability to deal with them. The teacher is like a demi-god in the eyes of children. What he says sometimes carries greater weight with them than what the parents have to say on a particular issue. Instances are not unknown where children quote their teachers against their parents. Cognitive development is as important at this stage as at any other stage. But the other aspects of training count for a lot more. In this situation, therefore, objectives have to be defined accordingly.

At the secondary stage, to a large extent, children have learnt to concentrate. A teacher teaches not only the subject that he is handling but also the principles of study and concentration. The teacher is no longer a demi-god but he is a force to be reckoned with nonetheless. Children find it difficult to ignore their teachers. They act as instructed and for the most part obey their teachers. Things begin to change somewhat when they move from the secondary to the higher secondary stage. But the mould is pre-set and even if they tend to be rebellious, children do not find it possible to be rebellious. This is also the stage when the process of looking upon the teachers as models gets under way. Girls sometimes have a crush on their teachers and boys not unoften idolise them.

A big change occurs when they enter college. Boys and girls of that age have much more confidence in their powers and capabilities. They do not accept everything at face value. Whether they question what they are told publicly or not, they are certainly sceptical. In several cases they express their scepticism openly. The inner state of defiance manifests itself in open rebellion also sometimes. Not only are students in a position to sit in judgement on their teachers, they actually do so. It is at this stage, more than at any other stage, that they resent the lack of fairness in dealing with them and openly question the pretence of their teachers, some of whom cannot live without them and are indeed addicted to them.

The objectives of teaching at this stage, therefore, have to be much more sharply defined. There are two broad divisions which must be kept in mind at this stage. At the undergraduate level, the intellectual objectives are to impart knowledge to students in their chosen disciplines and to enable them to think coherently. This is not the stage where, except in a few cases, they can do original thinking. That they should be able to think clearly and coherently is something that must be worked for and ensured. In most colleges in our country this does not happen. Intellectually, a large number of students at the undergraduate stage still continue to live in their higher secondary world. In terms of potential talent this is highly wasteful.

At the postgraduate stage the objectives have to undergo a change. Only 10-11 per cent of those who do their graduation go on to do postgraduate work. Even though, 90 per cent do not pursue the postgraduate course, it does not follow that those alone who are properly qualified go on to postgraduate study. Only a small percentage out of them come up to the required standard. At this stage the students are expected to think for themselves. Not many of them can do this and this is what explains the low level of performance at the postgraduate level.

In concrete terms, postgraduate students must be able to achieve two things. One, with every day that passes, there must be a sense of progression on their part. Every new addition to knowledge should get integrated with whatever they already know and should make them feel intellectually more competent. This, in turn, should enable them to think more coherently and more deeply.

Two, this flows from the first requirement, every postgraduate student must get a sensation of having his mind stretched and made more supple. Unless something of this kind happens, the objectives of postgraduate education are not fulfilled. Unfortunately, this does not happen in a very large number of cases. This is not the occasion to analyse the causes. Only one thing must be recognised: the cycle of poor and devitalised teaching and incompetent learning has been at work for more than a quarter century now. One does not see any signs of the cycle being broken at any stage. This is a cause for serious disquiet. For, apart from everything else, it causes confusion in respect of the objectives of teaching.

By the time a student is ready to undertake research he must be in a position to think for himself. It is the training of his mind and sensibility which constitute the bedrock of his education. Considering the fact that there is a lag at every stage, students who get down to research are clearly unequal to it in most cases. No wonder what they do is generally unsatisfactory and poor in quality.

It should not be necessary to analyse the situation any further in detail. Every teacher functions within a given social and cognitive framework. When the situation turns unfavourable on the social plane, there is little that the teacher can do. He himself is to some extent a victim of what is happening. On the cognitive plane he can do much more; for that is his own sphere of action. He feels defeated here also because nothing works according to plan and the objectives which ought to be followed at different stages of education are not always followed.

Meanwhile, the quality of those who go into teaching has not shown any improvement. A certain degree of decline has to be observed in the country. Social indiscipline and intellectual laxity have both combined to undermine the ethos of the profession. Sometimes the situation looks so depressing that one wonders what was the point about having been a teacher if this is all that one has been able to accomplish.

16
Teaching History to Undergraduates in India: A Trans-Indian View

W.H. McLEOD

WHEN I first went to India in 1958 it was to teach English in a higher secondary school in the Punjab. It was evidently assumed that because English was my mother tongue and because I possessed a university degree I should have little difficulty in serving as an effective teacher. The moment of truth came when I concluded my exposition of 'An Elegy on the Death of a Mad Dog'. During the exposition I had made it abundantly clear (so I imagined) that the pious man ironically described by Goldsmith was in fact a humbug and a hypocrite. Finally we came to the punch-line:

> The man recovered of the bite;
> The dog it was that died.

Blank incomprehension was the result. Why should the dog have died? I recognised that my capacities as a teacher of English to Punjabi school-boys were, to say the least, distinctly limited.

There were several reasons for this debacle. An obvious one was the fact that I was still speaking English with a strong New Zealand accent, an accent which my pupils often found difficult to understand. More important was the fact that English was not really my subject. More important still was my complete lack of training and experience as a teacher.

The solution which I adopted was a return to History (the subject in which I had graduated) and a change to the teaching of university undergraduates. Everyone knows that university teachers receive no training. Their role as lecturers evidently does not require it and armed with my postgraduate qualifications I was as well equipped on paper as most others. For the next four years I taught Punjabi history to undergraduates in a small college affiliated to Punjab University. Language was no longer a problem as I had developed a combination of Punjabi and English which seemed to serve the purpose adequately and which doubtless provided the few light moments in my lectures.

The role of a lecturer in these circumstances was difficult in some respects, easy in others. It was difficult in terms of the substantial number of classes each lecturer was expected to conduct, but easy in that there was little written work to mark. I merely had to speak for the appointed time, leaving the students to record as much as they wished. My only supplementary technique was one which I had learnt as an undergraduate in Dunedin. On one occasion the lecture had been delivered by a visiting American professor who arrived early and wrote an outline of his lecture on the blackboard. For me at least it proved to be very helpful and I have used the technique throughout my university teaching career. To avoid the rush and repetition of writing outlines before every lecture I typed them onto stencils and distributed a copy to each student.

I have no idea how effective these lectures were. My students were far too polite to offer any critical comments and I had never heard of course-evaluation questionnaires. Even the final examination results gave me no clear indication. The examinations were externally administered and I was well aware that after my lectures were completed the students made extensive use of 'bazar guides' in preparing themselves for their ordeal. These books were based on the well-founded assumption that each examination paper in History would include several stock questions drawn from a limited range of possibilities. Students who memorised model answers to these questions could feel reasonably secure and bazar guides provided them with that sense of security. Occasionally students would indicate that my time would be better spent dictating model answers. Could I, for example, give them the authoritative word on whether Guru Nanak was a reformer or a revolutionary!

There were thus two substantial problems which confronted me during those first four years of my career as a university teacher. The first was the system within which I had to teach, and the second was my lack of training. It was by no means a unique experience, though obviously it must have been complicated by the foreigner's ignorance of his students' backgrounds and of local conventions. All teachers at undergraduate colleges in the Punjab worked within the same system and the vast majority (as in most other countries) did so without the benefit of formal training.

II

Since leaving India I have taught undergraduates in three other countries, each with a different university system, different kinds of students, and radically different expectations as far as teaching methods are concerned. The bulk of my subsequent experience has been gained from teaching undergraduates at the University of Otago in New Zealand. Here I found myself teaching History in a conventional style within a system which involved both lecturing to large classes and seminars or tutorials with smaller groups. This was preceded by a period at the University of Sussex where each of my classes consisted of no more than two students and where most of my time was spent teaching the meaning of history by concentrating on a single book. The New Zealand experience was also supplemented by six months at the University of California in Berkeley, an experience which produced a different range of contrasts and taught a rather different lesson.

In a sense the Sussex experience was unrelated to my earlier teaching and only partly relevant to that which lay ahead. No one who teaches undergraduate History in either India or New Zealand expects to deal routinely with classes consisting of only two students. In two respects, however, the Sussex interlude produced a transforming effect.

One substantial benefit was the practical value of small-group teaching, a feature which most lecturers must surely appreciate but one which had hitherto eluded me in terms of actual experience. The Sussex procedure cannot be imitated in countries with staff/student ratios such as those one encounters in both India and New Zealand, but this does not mean that small-group teaching must necessarily be discarded as a workable method. I shall return to this point later.

The second benefit of the Sussex experience was the manner in which it so substantially enlarged my understanding of the historiographical component of History teaching. I do not know who developed the Sussex style of inducting first-year students into the Humanities and Social Sciences, nor do I know whether the same admirable system is still applied there. Indeed, I am not even sure that I fully understood it at the time or that I now recollect it accurately. It may be that my impressions represent, in some measure, a selective and idealised version of what the system was actually intended to achieve and of how it was actually applied. What I do know is that my perceptions, accurate or misconceived, made a very considerable impression on my understanding of History teaching and that I have ever since endeavoured to apply those insights to the different circumstances which I have subsequently encountered.

According to my recollection of the Sussex system all students who planned to graduate in Humanities or Social Sciences were required to devote the first two terms of their first year to History and Philosophy. During the first term half of the new students took a course entitled 'An Introduction to History' while the remainder took 'An Introduction to Philosophy'. During the second term they switched courses, thus covering both introductions. One of the benefits of the system was that it provided enlarged employment opportunities for lecturers with qualifications in History or Philosophy. Rather more substantial were the benefits which the two courses conferred on the students who were required to take them *and* on the lecturers who were required to teach them.

For the introductory course in History lecturers were given a choice of three books, any one of which was to form the basis for their own presentation of the subject. The three options were Burkhardt's *The Civilization of Renaissance in Italy*, Turner's *The Frontier in American History*, and Tawney's *Religion and the Rise of Capitalism.* The choice may actually have been made by some higher authority as I do not recollect actually deciding that mine would be Tawney, but at least it was the book which I would have wanted to teach and I greatly enjoyed doing so.

The purpose of the study thus thrust upon Sussex students was not that they should simply learn what Tawney had written with regard to the role of religion in the development of western capitalism. It was also intended that they should discover why he had chosen the topic, how he had researched and written it, and what interpretations he had embodied in the result. We began, as I recollect, by investigating the sources which Tawney had used. Within a short space of time we found that he had been reading Weber and indeed that *Religion and the Rise of Capitalism* was, in considerable measure, a commentary on the *The Protestant Ethic and the Spirit of Capitalism.* We paused to absorb Weber, soon discovering that neither he nor Tawney himself made much sense until we understood something of Marx and his theory of history.

While thus grappling with the conflicting interpretations of history which underlay Tawney's work we were also endeavouring to identify the actual sources from which he drew the materials for his own attempt to supply an acceptable theory. As we proceeded on through the book we found ourselves being drawn into a critical evaluation of the results which he was delivering, and our growing uneasiness with some of the evident inconsistencies prompted a closer study of the man himself. Some of the weaknesses of the book seemed plainly to derive from worthy ideals which somehow deflected the logic of his argument. Could these be explained by his own nurture and earlier commitment to a particular variety of humanitarian concern? We decided that this would probably be a legitimate conclusion to draw, thus learning to appreciate that when one studies an important work of historical interpretation one needs more than the words of the actual book itself. We also learnt that a work of history consists of much more than facts, and inevitably we found ourselves floundering as we attempted to define the distinction between fact and interpretation.

I am not sure how much my few Sussex students gained from

our Tawney exploration, but my impression is that the approach which the university prescribed succeeded in greatly enriching their understanding. It certainly enlarged mine and lessons which I learnt during my brief period at the University of Sussex have remained an integral part of my History teaching ever since. They underline much of what I shall subsequently say concerning the nature of historiography as an essential component in any undergraduate History course.

III

The Berkeley experience was rather different in that it taught me much more about the differing backgrounds of undergraduate students than about the interpretation of history. The first contact with my class of second-year students at the University of California in Berkeley was a little unnerving. They were so much more articulate than my Otago students that I actually had difficulty in getting through my lecturing plan. With a perfectly natural courtesy they were forever interrupting me with questions, objections, comments, suggestions, more questions. Never before had I encountered such an alert class and having adapted my planning I was able to enjoy their participation. If only, I thought, my Otago students would be as forthcoming.

This early experience with the class ill prepared me for what was to follow. When I began to mark their first written assignment I felt sure that there must be some mistake. The essays which I was reading could not possibly be the work of those bright, articulate, coherent students who sat in my class and contributed so much to its content and flow. But they were indeed the same students. What I was discovering was that although the Berkeley students could easily outdistance their Otago counterparts in oral expression a comparison of their written work produced a dramatic reversal in their ranking. The Otago students were producing essays and other written assignments which were considerably more mature in terms of content, organisation and English expression. My impression at the time was that the Otago students were at least two years ahead of the Berkeley students. This involved a nice irony in that back at the

University of Otago we were forever complaining about the weakness of the written work which our students submitted.

There was little that I could do about the written skills of Berkeley's students, but at least I could learn much from them with regard to oral participation. Although I was already aware of the value of verbal skills I had been inclined to accept that we were already doing as much as we could reasonably be expected to achieve in this area. The Berkeley experience persuaded me that a more determined effort was needed back at the University of Otago. It was not easy, and it remains difficult. Our schools deliver to the universities students who are unwilling to open their mouths in the presence of their peers and who still seem to think that education consists of acting as receptors of information dispensed by a person who stands at the front of the class.

A significant measure of teaching success is thus the capacity to open firmly-sealed lips and for this purpose most of us have to develop a range of conscious strategies. One which I have found useful is to learn the names of all the students in my classes. Given the size of some of our classes this is often a large task and few of us can claim to have succeeded in all instances. It is, nevertheless, a useful advantage for the lecturer who seeks to involve his students in open questioning and discussion. Another technique which achieves some success with New Zealand students (until they see through it) is to subject them to mild insult. This may well prompt a response, particularly when the insult concerns their home town or the school which they attended.

IV

These styles and strategies concern the teaching of History to New Zealand students and they are not the principal object of this report on experience. My principal object at this point concerns the question of how subsequent experience may have changed my approach. What difference has the experience made? If I were to return to undergraduate teaching in India what changes would I introduce into my teaching method?

The question, so easily put, is actually a very difficult one to answer. If I possessed the power to change the system it would perhaps be easier to answer, though the response would not necessarily be a very useful one. The last thing India needs is foreigners who tell her how to reorganise her university system. It is a system which the foreigner at least must accept. If he is to offer comment on teaching technique he must begin by accepting the current context within which that teaching is to be conducted. In the case of History teaching that means accepting an undergraduate examination system which still encourages the learning of model answers. It also involves competition from teachers who exploit the system with techniques which look suspiciously like rote learning.

Accepting the prevailing examination system does not mean, however, that one must resort to dictated information or succumb to model answers. Although undergraduates may still be comparatively immature in terms of learning skills they should be entering the stage where those skills increasingly become their own responsibility. They should also be entering the stage where increasingly they realise that history is not simply a matter of memorising an approved selection of facts. It involves differing interpretations, debate, and eventually personal choices. This should not suggest that they are to be treated as advanced postgraduates with a sophisticated understanding of research method and historiography. What it does suggest is that they should be introduced to reading and discussion which point them in that direction. At the same time they should be supplied with information of the kind which will enable them to cope with the examinations which eventually they must face.

This theory may perhaps be regarded as a compromise. If so, the description is just. It is unrealistic to expect that one can divorce the teaching and learning processes from the examination system which independently assesses those processes. Failure must be the certain result. The ideal, however, must be kept alive and it must be nourished in the hope that it will grow. Each generation of students is entitled to the best that the system can deliver and if that involves compromise none of us should be surprised.

What would be the nature of this compromise? There are five changes which I would adopt in my approach to teaching were I to return to undergraduate instruction in India. Two of them may seem comparatively trivial. The other three will perhaps appear more substantial.

The first of the apparently trivial items relates to the actual technique of teaching. Were I to be put back in a Punjabi lecture room I should ensure that I was accompanied by an overhead projector. For me personally this particular piece of simple technology has been far from trivial. Properly used it can have a significant effect on the order, clarity, and general appeal of a lecture presentation. Adding colour and variety it can present visual supplements without any interruption in the actual presentation. These include such obvious aids as maps and charts. They can also include key words and ideas, reinforcing statements which may be missed if one depends exclusively on oral delivery. No degree of blackboard skill can match the competent use of an overhead projector, and although there will always be charismatic lecturers who hold the attention of an audience without any visual aids such people are rare and their techniques ought never to be regarded as attainable by the majority of university teachers.

An obvious objection to the overhead projector is, of course, cost. Expense may well inhibit their general introduction, but it need not prohibit them altogether. They are simple instruments and in a society already well supplied with television sets they should not be treated as too costly. Their effective use by a few lecturers will quickly persuade others that they should be more generally available for the subjects to which they are particularly suited. I cannot believe that all college managements are so poor that they are quite unable to consider purchasing such elementary items.

Needless to say, this should not suggest that the delivery of an overhead projector into a lecturer's hands will automatically produce a dramatic improvement in teaching technique. On the contrary, it will usually produce a marked deterioration if delivery of the actual article is not accompanied by preliminary instruction in its use and by subsequent monitoring over a period of several weeks. This provides an elementary illustration of the need which should be served by the first of the three main suggestions. University lecturers who are to use overhead projectors need instruction in their use. The point can and should be generalised. University lecturers need instruction in the technique of teaching, not simply in the operating of a new piece of educational technology but in all aspects of the art. Indeed, the requirement can be pressed still further. University teachers need both preliminary and continuing exposure to training in teaching techniques and to regular participation in discussions concerning their role as teachers.

Does this mean that university lecturers should be formally trained in teachers' colleges prior to receiving their first appointments? Although many would benefit greatly from the experience it would be difficult to argue that the need justifies an investment on this scale. Besides, we are not going to get it. We must always work within the bounds of the attainable, and routine teacher college training for university lecturers does not fall within those bounds. The most that could be secured would be a short induction course and this is best conducted within the university itself.

It is within the universities and their affiliated colleges that the task should be tackled, and let no one suggest that it is necessarily impracticable. It is impracticable only where a college principal or a substantial majority of staff members believe it to be impracticable and treat it as such. In present circumstances it might be unrealistic to expect Indian universities to appoint staff to positions which would require them to work full time on the training of lecturers; and even if possible it would not necessarily be wise. In theory it should certainly be possible for a university to appoint a person to conduct training programmes in affiliated colleges, but in practice it is extraordinarily difficult to find individuals with appropriate skills sufficient to command respect who are prepared to renounce their own subjects in favour of educational development. The task, if it is to be performed, demands a cooperative effort on the part of a teaching staff, prodded by at least one enthusiastic member and sincerely supported by the college principal.

The combination of a dedicated yet tactful organiser, a sympathetic principal, and a potentially willing staff should make a regular lecturer-training programme possible. Discussion groups can be held at which experienced lecturers share their experience, prompting imitation where they have succeeded and discreet rejection where they have failed. Lecturers with particular skills (including visitors from other institutions) can be invited to conduct seminars. The teachers of particular subjects can organise their own subsidiary programmes. New staff members who are taking up their first appointments can be placed under the supervision of an experienced teacher able and prepared to give guidance throughout the first year. In smaller institutions occasional staff meetings can be devoted to discussing selected problems of education.

The fact that such seminars and discussions so often seem disappointingly inadequate does not mean that this is necessarily the case. At the very least they can keep alive an awareness of need, and often they will contribute useful ideas and information in the midst of much that is palpably futile. It is important that they should be built into the regular routine of the college or university and that they should not involve the kind of mandatory demands which create resentment. If one depends upon a permanently high level of enthusiasm the programme will assuredly dwindle and soon disappear.

V

The second of my main suggestions brings us back to the actual technique of teaching. It is a suggestion which may likewise be regarded as impracticable in the Indian undergraduate situation, yet it is one which must surely be attempted wherever a teaching method relies exclusively on lectures. I come to the first of the lessons which I learnt at the University of Sussex and which I have since endeavoured to apply at the University of Otago. Small-group teaching is essential in a subject such as History if the material is to be adequately presented and the individual student is to develop an appropriate range of skills.

It will obviously be impossible to introduce one-to-one teaching at the undergraduate level and given the demands imposed by existing staff/student ratios teaching groups of eight or ten students could impose serious strains on staff members who already find their lecturing schedule quite tiring enough. It is, however, unrealistic to imagine that students will grow to intellectual maturity within a system which relies exclusively on lectures as a teaching method. A few fortunate or determined students will achieve it by virtue of privileged circumstances, persistent curiosity, or self-disciplined study. The majority will emerge with a qualification which has little to do with sound learning, adequate skills, or the capacity to think independently.

The small seminar or tutorial group can serve several purposes. It can provide a far more effective structure for an essay-writing programme than the large lecture class. The latter compels the marker to rely on written comments, and because these are invariably so very time-consuming the result is usually either scant comment or a complete abandonment of essay-writing. Total abandonment is disastrous in a History department and if a tutorial group can provide an effective means of comment on an essay it can be justified for this reason alone.

Other justifications can also be offered. An obvious one is that the tutorial group provides precisely that opportunity to question and discuss which the lecture method so effectively inhibits. Because it should encourage questioning and discussion the small group can also serve the vital purpose of developing oral skills. Needless to say, the necessary response is not easily elicited from many students and the experience of small-group teaching should quickly reinforce the need for the training of lecturers. If, however, students are denied the opportunity to engage in structured discussion the value of their education is seriously diminished.

Lectures, written assignments and small-group discussions may seem an unexciting and drearily conventional approach to undergraduate teaching. Personally I am convinced that all three are essential and that a system which lacks any of the three is seriously crippled. A system which relies exclusively on lectures as a means of undergraduate education in the Humanities or Social Sciences must be regarded as alarmingly inadequate and drastically in need of supplements.

The supplements may, of course, be very difficult to secure.

Heavy lecturing loads leave little time for marking written assignments or for conducting tutorial groups, and staff members who have grown accustomed to a professional life lived exclusively in the lecture room will not necessarily be enthused by the suggestion that their activities should be diversified. This lack of enthusiasm is likely to be strengthened by the actual experience of small-group teaching, an experience which can so convincingly demonstrate our limited skills as teachers and which at times can be positively humiliating. And yet the diverse range is essential if undergraduate teaching is to be truly effective. The most expensive selection of audio-visual aids cannot provide an adequate substitute, nor can the most compelling charisma. If our students are not trained to express themselves orally and on paper (whether by pen or by keyboard) their education must fall far short of a minimum acceptable standard.

The stress on oral and written presentation should concern all subjects within the general area of the Humanities and Social Sciences. My third main change concerns only the teaching of History. In a sense it is not a change because it involves a lesson which I learnt from a colleague while teaching in India and which I endeavoured to apply at the time. Subsequent experience has significantly reinforced the value of the lesson and has also indicated other ways in which it can be applied. It is here that the second Sussex boon has proven to be so valuable.

The lesson which I learnt from my colleague concerns the need for formal instruction in historical interpretation as a part of any undergraduate syllabus in History. The correct term is historiography and I am still not sure why I attempt to avoid it. (When I introduced my own paper in the subject at the University of Otago I called it 'An Introduction to Historical Method and Interpretation', preferring a cumbersome title to the single sufficient word.) It may perhaps be a fear of jargon or of academic pretension which inhibits my use of the word, but historiography is what I mean and historiography I hold to be a vital component in any History syllabus.

There are, I believe, two axioms to be enunciated in this connection. The first is that all historical studies involve interpretation. The second is that students of History are congenitally blind to the moulding influence of interpretation in the presentation of historical facts and to their acceptance by readers or hearers. It is the second axiom which justifies the incorporation of historiography within a History syllabus at the university level. The fact that it is so often absent may perhaps suggest that many teachers suffer from the same blindness, or at least that they do not perceive the all pervading influence of interpretation with sufficient clarity.

Many teachers, however, would offer a different explanation for the omission. It is that the Indian undergraduate student is not yet sufficiently mature to cope with the sophisticated demands of formal historiography and that the appropriate place for its introduction is the graduate level. Graduate classes in historiography are vastly better than none at all and I have been impressed by the work being done in this area by the History Department at Guru Nanak Dev University in Amritsar. I do not agree, however, that we must delay their introduction until this advanced stage. What I do accept is that we are confronted yet again with the need to compromise. It is unrealistic to expect that undergraduate syllabuses will be amended to include the formal study of interpretation in History. The teacher who acknowledges the need must therefore incorporate it within his or her presentation of the routine syllabus required at each stage.

Teachers who accept and apply this conclusion will necessarily pace their students, introducing discussion and explanation which are appropriate to the students' level of understanding. Although no student who deserves a place in a college is too immature for elementary historiography some entrants will certainly ensure that it does need to be elementary at the initial stage. Thereafter it should grow in sophistication as the undergraduate moves through the various levels of a B.A. degree. If it can be taught in a small-group situation so much the better, for each need will serve the other. Historiographical issues can stimulate discussion; and discreetly directed discussion should help develop a student's capacity for critical thought and expression.

I began with one of the apparently trivial items and I conclude with the other. As with the first it is anything but trivial, either for the value which it confers or for the difficulties which it involves. It concerns the lesson which I learnt in Berkeley. The quality of History teaching (and of many other subjects) is greatly enhanced by active student participation. Oral contributions from students should be encouraged, regardless of how large the class may be.

I am well aware that these proposals will impress many people as fine ideals, as principles which may be eminently suited to the undergraduate situation in a New Zealand university. But try applying them in a small college in the Punjab and see how long they last. One response is that staff/student ratios are not so wondrously generous in New Zealand and that the pursuit of ideals needs persistence there as anywhere else. The other response (the more relevant one) is that the need for compromise is fully recognised. Ideals which one seeks to apply always get tarnished in the process. The tarnish need not mean that the ideals have lost all their use and value. Sensible compromise is far removed from outright rejection and if we compromise with positive rather than negative or resigned intent then assuredly we are still on the path of progress.

Index

Administrator, experience of a teacher as, 23-25, 56-58, 74
Ahmed, Rais, 9
All My Sons, 117
An Intensive Course in English, 114
Antigone, 117
Aquinas, Thomas, 153
Aristotle, 108
Armond, 136
Armoury Raid 1930, 15
Art of Teaching, 169

Bagchi, Amiya, 21
Banaras Hindu University, teaching experience at, 133-34
Banerjee, Dipak, 21
Banerjee, Surendranath, 16
Bhattacharya, Dhires, 21
Bisi, Pramathanath, 16
Bose, Buddhadeva, 16
Boyd, A.J., 82
Buddha, 103
Burkhardt, 193

Chakravarti, Phani Bhusan, 14
Chakravarti, Sukhamoy, 21
Chatterjee, Nripendra, 16
Civilization of Renaissance in Italy, 193
Co-education, 146-47
Coyajee, Jehangir, 14

Datta, Ajit, 16
De Mann, Paul, 154
Delhi School of Economics, teaching experience at, 30-46
Delhi School of Social Work, teaching experience at, 72-78
Delhi University, teaching experience at, 60-69
Derrida, Jacques, 152
Dey, Bishnu, 16
Dustoor, P.E., 113
Dutt, Palme, 81

Economics, relevance of teaching, 79-97
Eddington, 71
Education, stages of, 187-89
Engineering, teaching of, 131-41
Evans-Pritchard, 37
Executive Thinking and Action, 136
Experience of a teacher at,
    as administrator, 23-25, 56-58, 74
    Banaras Hindu University, 133-34
    Delhi School of Economics, 30-46
    Delhi School of Social Work, 172-78
    Delhi University, 60-69
    Hans Raj College, 106-19
    Hindu College, 47-57
    Indira Gandhi National Open University (IGNOU), 169-72
    as an individual, 27-29
    Madras Christian College (MCC), 82-97
    Patna University, 59-60
    Presidency College, 19-23
    Ripon College, 15-19
    in search of relevance, 79-97
    Sydney Law School, 152-58
    as Vice-Chairman, 76-78
    University of Roorkee, 132-41
    as a women, 142-49

Fish, Stanely, 155
Frontier in American History, 193
Gandhi, M.K., 71, 103

Ganguli, B.N., 32, 34
Ghosal, Upendranath, 20
Ghosh, Nandalal, 16
Ghosh, Prafulla Chandra, 14
Ghosh, Rabindra Narayan, 16
Gobind Ram, 116, 119
Goel, Suresh, 160
Goldsmith, 190
Gwyer, Maurice, 50

Hamlet, 115
Hans Raj College, teaching experience at, 106-19
Heart of Aryavarta, 14
Highet, G., 169
Hindu College, teaching experience at, 47-57
History, teaching of, 190-204
Hogg, A.G., 82
Homer, 116
House, Humphry, 16
Hussain, Zakir, 12

Ilaksha, 119
India Today, 81
Indian Education—A Primer for Reformers, 105
Indira Gandhi National Open University (IGNOU), teaching experience at, 169-72

Jalan, Bimal, 21
John, V.V., 113

Kalidas, 110, 116
Karam Chand, 115
Kothari, D.S., 30, 53
Kothari Commission, 87

Lalaji, 119
Lindsay, A.D., 82

Macbeth, 117
Madras Christian College (MCC), experience of teaching at, 82-97
Mahaveer, 103
Majumdar, Tapas, 20
Malthus, 25
Marshall, 25, 90
Marx, 194
Matthew, 113, 119
Maugham, 71
Maunica, 118
Mehta, R.S., 113
Michael, 118
Miller, Arthur, 117
Miller, William, 82
Milton, 118
Model teacher, 183-84
Much Ado, 117
Mukherjee, Asutosh, 13
Mukherjee, Hiren, 16

Nehru, Jawaharlal, 71
Niyogi, Jitendra Prasad, 14

Optimum, 25
Our India, 80

Paradise Lost, 118-19
Patna University, teaching experience at, 59-60
Plato, 108
Plautus, 117
Pot of Gold, 117
Presidency College, teaching experience at, 19-23
Principles of Economics, 90
Protestant Ethic and the Spirit of Capitalism, 194

Rahman, Sheikh Mujibur, 19
Raj, K.N., 34, 107
Rajinder Pal, 109
Rajpal, 118
Rajpal Ravi, 119
Rakshit, Mihir, 21
Ramanuja, 103

Index

Rameshwar, 118
Rampu, 119
Rao, V.K.R.V, 30, 54
Religion and the Rise of Capitalism, 193-94
Research scholar-teacher relation, 39-41
Ripon College, teaching experience at, 15-19
Robinson, Joan, 25
Ronaldshay, 14
Roy, Birendra Benod, 16
Russel, 71

Sadler Commission, 13, 17
Sangeeta, 118
Sanjay, 118
Sarates, 113
Sarkar, Benoy Kumar, 14
Science, teaching of, 120-30
Scotus, Dunus, 153
Sen, Nabendu, 21
Seth, B.R., 47-48, 50-51
Shakespeare, 110, 116-17
Shankara, 103
Shanti Narayan, 107
Shaw, 71, 110
Shri Ram, 52
Singh, Atma, 116, 119
Singh, Baldev, 116, 119
Singh, Rajinder, 116
Singh, S.R., 109
Singh, Sarup, 114
Singh, Surjeet, 116
Sir Dorabji Tata Graduate School of Social Work, 72
Slater, Gilbert, 90
Socrates, 108
Sophocels, 110, 117
Srinivas, M.N., 32, 37, 39
Stalin, 44
Stone, Julius, 152
Student-teacher relation, 60-61, 73-78, 160-60, 177-82
Students Helping Association, 52
Successful teacher, 100-03
Summer school, 54
Sydney Law School, teaching experience at, 152-58

Tata Institute of Social Sciences, 76
Tawney, 193-94
Teacher,
   as a model, 183-84
   pleasure of being, 98-103, 173-89
   reasons for being a, 81-97
   research scholar relation, 39-41, 62-65
   secret of a successful, 100-03
   students relation, 60-61, 73-78, 160-70, 177-82
   women, 142-49
Teaching,
   administration and, 41-42
   as adventure, 12-29
   art of, 184-86
   authenticity in, 104-19
   as a career, 30-46
   as declining profession, 30-46
   of economics, 79-97
   of engineering, 131-41
   of history, 190-204
   objective of, 176-77
   party politics and, 43-45, 65-69
   problem in, 120-30
   as provocation, 150-58
   research work and, 62-65
   of science, 120-30
   sincerity in, 159-72
   with a cause, 70-78
Turner, 193

Undergraduates in India, teaching history to, 190-204
University of Roorkee, teaching experiece at, 132-41
University School of Economics and Sociology, Bombay, 72

Verma, K.G., 114
Verma, P.S., 114
Vice-Chancellor, experience of a teacher as, 76-78

Weber, 194

Wisconsin, 113
Women teacher, experience of, 142-49

You and Your Students, 56